W9-BKV-442

Kenneth Burke's Dramatism

Kenneth Burke's Dramatism and Popular Arts

C. Ronald Kimberling

Bowling Green State University Popular Press
Bowling Green, Ohio 43403

Library of Congress Catalog Card No. 81-85522

ISBN: 0-87972-195-2 Clothbound
       0-87972-196-0 Paperback

Copyright © 1982 Bowling Green University Popular Press

To Haesoon Yong Kimberling

Contents

Acknowledgments

This volume represents, in more ways than I can recall, the distillation of ideas planted by several master educators. Not the least among them is W. Ross Winterowd, whose enthusiasm for new ideas and mastery of the art of synthesis continually give me fresh hope for the academic enterprise. Dr. Winterowd deserves full credit for keeping me on course in this project. I am also grateful for the gentle criticism provided by Marjorie Perloff, who prevented the sections on *Jaws, Shogun* and *The Dead Zone* from being too isolated from the main body of Burke's thought. If Dr. Perloff helped keep my feet on the ground, John Orr, a world-wise theologian, can be credited with keeping my head in the clouds.

Several individuals have played an indirect role in the shape of this work by the various ways in which they have contributed to my intellectual development during the past decade. Ray Browne, Kenneth Devol, Luther Luedtke, Patrick Morrow, Hershel Parker and Joseph Webb are all deserving of special mention.

Then, of course, there's this funny little genius in New Jersey....

Introduction

The work which follows represents an effort to scratch an itch. The itch was my long-felt sense of frustration when I was confronted by those literary scholars who persisted in avoiding serious discussion whenever they encountered popular art. Even though they should have known better, these explicators of such popular writers as Shakespeare and Dickens seemed to crumble when faced with the popular art of their own age. Rather than admit they knew little about the complexities of punk rock, for example, these guardians of the canon would resort to *ad hominem* arguments about "plastic bubblegum music" and "commercial exploitation." Few cared to use their training in criticism to try to make sense of the popular fare of our times.

Though I may be overgeneralizing, I am setting up no straw men. Most "serious" critics do not take popular art seriously. How does one demonstrate to them—in terms they can relate to—that popular art is worth investigating? The present study is an essay with that purpose.

Kenneth Burke is my principal source. His theory of Dramatism provides me with a methodological instrument to investigate and unravel some of the mysteries shrouding the production and consumption of popular art. In the chapters which follow, I explicate Burke's methodology and apply it to some of the major questions concerning artistry, form and audience response in the popular arts.

The organizational scheme of this study follows the outline of traditional rhetoric. I first consider the artist, an examination of *ethos*, if you will. A study of form in popular culture follows next, in Chapter II. Audience response—*pathos*—is dealt with in Chapter III. Finally, in Chapter IV, I speculate briefly on the type of studies of popular art that may follow from a further application of Burke's ideas.

Throughout the study, I offer samples of "applied Dramatism," practical criticism of the popular arts designed to help demonstrate that Burke's is not an airy methodology but one that has something to say about real works of art present in the real world of men and women. Though the original sources are all novels, I have chosen a film (*Jaws*), a television miniseries (*Shogun)* and a popular novel *(The Dead Zone)* to help fend off those potential critics who might suggest that Dramatism fails to work for more than just the print medium. I hope I am forgiven for confining my critical voyages to the narrow straits and channels close to the land covered in a particular chapter. More adventurous sailings can hopefully be scheduled in the future, in a work less concerned with the development of an overall methodology.

I
Dramatism and Authorship
in Popular Art

Each of the methodological approaches to the study of popular arts which have been widely used in the past twenty years or so leaves out one or more elements crucial to the communications process. There are really two major activities to be examined in any work of fiction. The first involves the basic act of artistic creation and communication. The second involves content and structure: such matters as plot, theme and narrative technique. Thus, for example, Marshall McLuhan neglects content with his insistence on dealing solely with the effects of media upon audiences. Sociologist Herbert Gans focuses on the interaction between plot types and audiences, but he ignores the role of the artist in fashioning a work that appeals to different types of people.

In this study I have chosen to highlight a method that seems best suited for the task of addressing both the "outer" act of communication between artist and audience and the "inner" action of the work as it reflects authorial intention and as it captures the imagination of an audience. The "Dramatistic" method developed by Kenneth Burke fills the need for an instrument to develop both extrinsic and intrinsic criticism. Dramatism has the flexibility to enable us to penetrate several aspects of popular arts from a variety of angles; unlike much of the earlier criticism of popular arts, it is not steeped in the "ideological" paradigm of a single academic discipline. While it may not be the Ultimate Answer, Dramatism assuredly provides critical insights that cannot be generated by any other method.

Burke derives his methodology from the basic assumption

that human beings are divided from other members of the animal kingdom by virtue of their ability to communicate symbolically via language. As Burke defines us:

Man is
the symbol-using (symbol-making, symbol-misusing animal)
inventor of the negative (or moralized by the negative)
separated from his natural condition by instruments of his own making
goaded by the spirit of hierarchy (or moved by the sense of order)
and rotten with perfection.[1]

Here Burke suggests that we are qualitatively different from other animals by the fact that language enables us to build symbolic models that become a "scenic" reality, serving as a backdrop for our thoughts and experiences. This is not an idea original to Burke; the concept is basic to social anthropology, psychology, and several other disciplines. But Burke builds upon this insight, using it as the basis for a world-view wherein the major distinction is between *motion* and *action*. In Burke's universe things move, persons act. No symbolic transformation is involved when a rock rolls down a hill, gathering moss as it travels. But when I raise my wine glass to toast the good company at my table, something magical occurs. My act represents something for all who are present, and the essence of all human activity occurring within a social arena is best captured by a methodology that recognizes and reveals something about the interaction among the "imaginative worlds" of each guest as he or she is transformed by language.

Two possible philosophical premises may underlie such a methodology. One way to build such a system would be to start from epistemological assumptions, creating a system based upon how humans "know" the world. Another would be based on *praxis*, human action, with an emphasis on the study of motivated *behavior* over modes of consciousness. Burke chooses the latter approach, focusing on manners and motives instead of knowledge and understanding.

This is not to suggest that Dramatism is entirely without epistemological grounding. For Burke, human action has its roots in language, language being the most fundamental tool by which human beings symbolically convey their conceptions of reality to one another. As Burke notes:

> The method would involve the explicit study of language as the "critical moment" at which human motives take form, since a linguistic factor at every point in human experience complicates and to some extent transcends the purely biological aspects of motivation.[2]

Dramatism, as one might suppose, derives its name from the drama, where the crucial focus is upon *acts* performed by various players. Just as in a play, the act is central insofar as it reveals human motives. Dramatism employs a Pentad of terms used to provide a fundamental order by which we may examine linguistic transformations of experience. The Pentad consists of Act, Scene, Agent, Purpose and Agency. Each term stands in contrastive relationship to the other terms, yoked by a common ground or substance. As Burke notes, "Their participation in a common ground makes for transformability" (*Grammar*, p. xiii). Thus Burke tells us that the human body may be treated as a property of Agent by the portrait painter, since the artist focuses on the body as it expresses personality, while for the physician, the body serves as the Scene or material upon which medicine is practiced.

The terms are necessarily ambiguous because they are generative. Going back to Burke's basic axioms, we discover the need for a generative, ambiguous terminology. Action, as distinct from mere motion, involves human thought. Thought is centered in language, and language by its very nature involves symbolic transformation of the "raw" outer world. The best method for discussing human action, Burke argues, is not one based upon static terms, but rather one based upon the contrast and ambiguity inherent in language:

> We take it for granted that, insofar as men cannot themselves create the universe, there must remain something essentially enigmatic about the problem

> of motives, and that this underlying enigma will
> manifest itself in inevitable ambiguities and
> inconsistencies among the terms for motives.
> Accordingly, what we want is *not terms that avoid
> ambiguity,* but *terms that clearly reveal the strategic
> spots at which ambiguities necessarily arise.*
> *(Grammar,* pp. xii—xiii.)

Dramatism thus articulates a unique position in the age-old philosophical debate between subjectivists and objectivists. It is not that reality *per se* is subjective, Burke argues, but that human terms "enveloping" reality are unable to capture reality in its objective essence. We may recall that a key phrase in Burke's "definition of man" is "inventor of the negative." Language provides us with the means of knowing objects and events by way of contrast and variation. We may not agree upon what something *is,* but we agree upon what it *is not.*

By merging and dividing terms, we arrive at an understanding of human motives dialectically. Each term of the Pentad can be viewed in relationship to the other terms. Each term can also be transformed into another as the context or ground of our attention shifts; earlier we noted how the human body, ordinarily functioning as Agent, becomes the Scene for a physician. Burke asserts that:

> Distinctions, we might say, arise out of a great
> central moltenness, where all is merged. They have
> been thrown from a liquid center to the surface, where
> they have congealed. Let one of these crusted
> distinctions return to its source, and in this alchemic
> center it may be remade, again becoming molten
> liquid, and may enter into new combinations,
> whereat it may be again thrown forth as a new crust,
> a different distinction. *(Grammar,* p. xiii.)

Burke argues that each distinction travels back to "the ground of its existence, the logical substance that is its causal ancestor."

This concept of "substance" or "ground" (Burke uses these

terms interchangeably) is similar to what a phenomenologist means by the term "intentional object." It is the pure context surrounding the act, providing us with a framework within which our Dramatistic terminology may be applied. Burke notes that substance in and of itself is ironic because "though used to designate something *within* the thing, *intrinsic* to it, the word etymologically refers to something *outside* the thing, *extrinsic* to it" (*Grammar*, p. 23). A thing's context, surrounding it "extrinsically," is by definition that which the thing *is not*.

Thus Burke arrives at the concept of "dialectic substance," which

> derives its character from the systematic contemplation of the antimonies attendant upon the fact that we necessarily define a thing in terms of something else. "Dialectic substance" would thus be the over-all category of dramatism, which treats of human motives in terms of verbal action. (*Grammar*, p. 33)

Although Burke notes that human motives are not confined to the realm of verbal action, the Dramatistic method suggests that as a "point of departure" we engage in a systematic search for key terms. "Ancestral terms" are terms which reveal substance; "derivative terms" are terms which stand in some sort of rational relationship to ancestral terms, transforming them by revealing a multitude of terminological possibilities. "Act" is the ancestral term for the Dramatistic method, "a terministic center from which many related considerations can be shown to 'radiate,' as though it were a 'god term' from which a whole universe of terms is derived."[3]

We should not be fooled into imagining that Act is self-evident. The Pentad of Dramatistic terms must always be placed within a certain Circumference which circumscribes the stage upon which the drama is being acted out. As Michael George Feehan observes, "Circumference is Burke's term for the scope of the analytic enterprise, the range of interest, the breadth of the study to be undertaken."[4] Let us suppose, for example, that I am a middle-level manager in a large corporation. I have just fired an employee for being chronically tardy. The Act may be viewed in terms of the immediate situation: a man (manager) engages in the act of uttering certain words to another man ("You are fired!"). With a slightly larger Circumference, the Act may be defined as that of providing education about acceptable social roles; my firing the employee becomes mere "negative feedback." Enlarge the scope a bit more, and you may find an Act of victimage, engaged in by an Agent (me) wishing to enhance his position in the social hierarchy (the bureaucratic structure of the corporation). Alter the Circumference a bit more, and it becomes my failure to practice the Christian virtues of charity and humility. Clearly, Circumference provides a "container" which defines the boundaries of any Dramatistic analysis. We may enlarge the scope of any study to allow for a consideration of its "universal, timeless" implications, though generally speaking, we tend to examine a thing "in terms of" a more limited Scene.

The notion of Circumference reveals how interrelated are the terms of the Pentad. Acts occur within Scenes, though as we have noted in the example above, the Scene is not always self-evident. If we place my Act of firing the employee within a Scene involving two persons, the Act involves me as Agent. But if we widen the scope, the Agent may become the corporate hierarchy as a depersonalized entity, with both myself and the terminated employee serving as objects of an entirely different Act, the Act of an anonymous hierarchy working its inexorable will upon those within its compass.

Burke uses the term "ratio" to describe the interrelationships among terms. The dialectical method assumes that one of the five terms will be ancestral in a given situation, functioning heuristically to reveal the central motive. Closely linked to the ancestral term will be another term. In the example we have been using, Scene becomes the ancestral term, operating indissolubly with Act. As we enlarge or reduce the scope of the Scene, the Act shifts as well. The Dramatistic method can thus be described as an initial search for the ancestral term, followed by a determination of the term most closely associated with it. Within a given Circumference, the ancestral term has a certain effect upon the second term in the ratio. The method becomes a rounded heuristic by virtue of the twenty possible ratios existing among the five terms (Burke, however, discusses only ten ratios in *A Grammar of Motives*) as such ratios become possible, given alterations in Circumference.

A "Scene-Act ratio," for example, offers us insight into the way by which Scene influences and helps define the nature of the Act. An Act-Agent ratio looks at how the Act operates on the Agent. In our example of the employee being fired, we may examine the point of view of the corporate executive who looks at my Act of firing the employee as proof that I have the "strong fiber" required for higher-level management responsibility.

As a heuristic, Dramatism is open-ended. As Circumference is enlarged or reduced, each of the twenty ratios may be examined, and the nature of each term may shift radically. The effect is like that of a prism, bending rays of light in a variety of directions. What gives the method some focus, however, is the notion of substance. While not immediately apparent, substance can be "teased out" by the dialectical method of Dramatism. The terms involved in the *Grammar* reveal praxeological—if not epistemological—"reality." As Burke notes:

> To call a man a friend or brother is to proclaim him consubstantial with oneself, one's values or purposes. To call a man a bastard is to attack him by attacking his whole line, his "authorship," his "principle" or "motive" (as expressed in terms of the familial). An epithet assigns substance doubly, for in stating the character of the object it at the same time contains an implicit program of action with regard to the object, thus serving as motive. (*Grammar*, p. 57).

This passage reveals that a dialectical dynamic may be established between the five terms and the concept of substance itself. As Frehan notes: "With the introduction of

Circumference and Ratios, the Pentad clarifies the ways in which quality or value enters into linguistic transformations. Widening and narrowing scope, altering the direction of 'dominance,' changes the quality of motivations, resulting in 'transcendence'."[5]

It is this transcendental aspect of language that stands behind the whole project of Dramatism. The *Grammar* represents but a single aspect of a series tentatively titled "On Human Relations." The *Grammar* deals with "resources of placement" available to all persons as they epistemologically grapple with the external world. The *Rhetoric of Motives*, published in 1950, deals with partisan action, with the way in which we all identify with certain groups and interests. A *Symbolic of Motives* would deal with individuality, with the uniqueness of acts or forms. The *Symbolic* has not yet been published, though most of it has reportedly been written. An unanticipated addition to the project is *Language as Symbolic Action*, a collection of essays published in 1966, dealing with the suasive power of language as it directs human action apart from its location in a specific art. *LASA* thus treats language as a unique type of Agency.

Dramatism And Recent Popular Art Criticism

Thus armed with the basic tools of the Dramatistic method, we may pause before considering the role of artistry in the popular arts to discuss some of the methods used by recent popular arts critics—Dwight Macdonald, Marshall McLuhan, Herbert Gans and Abraham Kaplan—in terms of Burke's methodology. Seen from a Dramatistic perspective, each critic's approach has fundamental *lacunae*. It is the aim of the present study to provide the serious student of the popular arts with the tools to engage in a more rounded discussion of the topic than has occurred with the application of previous critical methods.

From a Dramatistic perspective, the fears that Dwight Macdonald and Ernest Van Den Haag expressed some twenty years ago about the popular arts creating a nation of mindless robots result from their begging the question at the very start of their analyses. In their views, popular (or "mass") art functions not as Scene, as one might ordinarily expect, but as Agency. "Masscult" itself is the force involved in the Act of brainwashing the public into accepting lower standards of art. This Act is accomplished with the "Sub-Agency" of modern electronic technology, the mass media. The question-begging occurs with respect to Scene. The Dramatistic model pinpoints the masscult critics' acceptance of a neo-Spenglerian "decline of the West" scenario as the key element behind their fear of the popular arts. Dramatism leads us to an "Act within an Act" wherein we see the hapless masscult critic, convinced that the world is going to seed, forced to engage in an earnest search for a "devil figure" responsible for all the gloom and doom. No "chief conspirator" can easily be found, but the critic does note that modern technology has provided the artist with new, electronic modes of communication. The Sub-Agency of electronic technology as well as the Agency of masscult in general grow to become the necessary devil figures, dangerous tools in the hands of those who unwittingly use them to destroy traditional Western civilization. While others may see a mere correlative relationship between the rise of popular art as transmitted by the electronic media and a "decline" in Western civilization, the masscult critics, feeling victimized, posit a cause/effect relationship between the two.

It is interesting that Edward Shils' response to the masscult critics employs the same premise, that popular art functions as an Agency in shaping the behavior of audiences.[6] In defending popular art, Shils merely enlarges the Circumference, taking a longer view of history. Given the fact that the masses have been illiterate for most of history, Shils argues, and given that *some* form of popular entertainment has always existed, the "massification" of information is actually a blessing. This enlargement of scope changes the nature of the Act. For the masscult critics, the Act is the "decline of the West" via the Agency of mass culture. For Shils, it is modern technology helping to overcome the ignorance and superstition of earlier ages. The Act thus becomes "edification and enlightenment" instead of "suppression of aesthetic excellence."

The usefulness of Dramatism as a tool to probe various critical methods is shown when we examine the views of Marshall McLuhan. McLuhan is generally thought to be an "original," a humanist whose ideas spring from unique premises. Yet the Dramatist readily sees that McLuhan stands close to the masscult critics in his focus upon the power of mass media as Agencies. McLuhan does differ in the sense that individual media are treated as primary Agencies, overshadowing the "Agency" of masscult conventions. To McLuhan, form is a function of medium, and content is irrelevant. Nevertheless, the emphasis in McLuhan's work is placed upon the power of mass media in creating specialized "response modes" for their audiences. The member of the audience is thus not someone who has an "appetency for content" and who enjoys the popular arts by virtue of having his or her expectations met by material presented in conventional forms, but rather someone who engages in a form of sensory reflex action in response to a particular medium. Dramatism reveals McLuhan as a closet behaviorist!

Another form of popular arts criticism to emerge during the Sixties and early Seventies represented an attempt on the part of sociologists to classify audience types. Partly this was an effort to counter the arguments of elitist critics with a plea for cultural pluralism; working toward this end, sociological critics tried to show that certain classes of people have an entirely different cultural orientation toward "art" than other classes. Any attempt to force the values and standards of one class upon another would be a form of tyranny. According to this argument, popular art has legitimacy because it has a rightful place in a cultural heterodoxy.

Perhaps the most widely known proponent of this view is Herbert J. Gans, whose *Popular Culture and High Culture* attempts to define five major "taste cultures" representing different segments of the American public.[7] Gans' principal concern is to establish a typology of culture creators and consumers and to outline their shared value structures. Unlike the rhetorician, Gans is more interested in exploring the group identifications of the various culture-consuming publics than he is in analyzing the acts of creating and experiencing works of popular art.

There are five basic taste cultures, according to Gans: high culture, upper-middle culture, lower-middle culture, low culture and quasi-folk low culture. The principal differences among the five lie in creator versus user orientation, preferences for art works conveyed by different media, and the degree of abstraction (as opposed to mimesis) present in works of art designed for particular taste cultures. Participants in the first four taste cultures can be typed according to education and socioeconomic status within a broadly defined American "national" culture, while quasi-folk low culture consists of unamalgamated ethnic groups whose lack of integration into a national culture has managed to preserve many unadulterated elements of provincial or foreign folk culture. The term "taste culture" refers to creators, audiences and critics who all share the same set of values and the same attitude toward art; Gans reserves the term "taste *public*" to refer to the audience for works of art produced by each of the taste cultures.

In this model of various "taste publics," the sociologist engages in a type of criticism that stresses the Act of culture consumption. The Agent in Gans' model is the member of the audience, functioning as a consumer of various cultural products. Gans' theory of taste cultures, with corresponding taste publics, is really a theory outlining the Scene within which culture consumption occurs. A member of a particular taste public identifies with a particular cultural product, whether it is "Barney Miller" or Beethoven's Ninth Symphony, for the Purpose of achieving consubstantiality with other members of the taste public. Patterns of culture consumption become "badges" which identify someone as a member of a particular taste public.

The main problem with Gans' model is its failure to go beyond the Act of consumption. The Act performed by the artist, producing the work of art, is completely ignored.

Moreover, in terming popular art "user-oriented" and high art "creator-oriented," Gans seems to be suggesting that works of art have certain properties which inherently stimulate particular types of responses. With authorial intention left out of the picture, all works of art are presented as having some sort of "mystical" propensity to attract certain audiences.

Elsewhere, however, Gans goes to great lengths to demonstrate how the different modes of response displayed by the different taste publics are explained by sociological factors such as education and income. Clearly, Gans is confused in trying to explain how works of art and different types of audiences "match up" with each other. If the match results from properties inherent in the work of art, we are back to the behaviorist model. If it results from sociologically differentiated audiences "shopping" for art which appeals to the appetites of these different taste groups, we find ourselves examining significantly different art *products* with no mention of the Agents (artists) whose awareness of these differences in taste led to the production of different types of art geared to different types of audiences. Surely Gans cannot attribute the differences in art to differences in audience makeup; to do so would be to suggest that the audience is the "real" artist.

Overall we find that Gans' model is limited in scope, reducing the overall Scene from one wherein multiple Acts of communication and response occur to one focusing solely on response. By leaving out any discussion of the artist as Agent, he denies himself the opportunity to examine how artists anticipate how their audiences will react, and how this anticipation plays a significant role in the Act of *creating* a work of popular art. Additionally, by excluding the artist, Gans categorically denies himself the opportunity to examine any "creator-oriented" component in the audience's interplay with works of popular art.

Finally, we may look at what the Dramatist would have to say about the aesthetic approach of Abraham Kaplan as presented in his widely circulated essay "The Aesthetics of the Popular Arts."[8] Kaplan distinguishes between an aesthetic "response" to high art and an affective "reaction" triggered by popular art. The response is "cognitive" calling into play the power of the imagination as it grapples with the work of art, while the reaction is "affective," involving the placement of the work of popular art into a conventional type category. The distinction suggests two different Acts, both involving the work of art as Agency. The primary difference is in the Scene within which a member of the audience is placed. For popular art, the Scene is rather mechanistic, the work of art simply "setting up" some sort of culturally conditioned pattern of behavior. For high art, we find an enlarged scope, whereby the work of art stimulates more complex Acts of imaginative interplay on the part of the audience. Thus to the Dramatist, Kaplan's aesthetic is dependent upon an adjustment of the Circumference.

Kaplan's underlying premise is that art should always serve the normative Purpose of promoting the development of the individual. Such growth is placed within a Scene whereby the member of the audience must use a work of art as a tool (Agency) in sorting out values, attitudes and modes of being. Acts wherein the audience simply recognizes and affirms a "true-to-life" quality in the work ("Yes, this villain is just like my uncle, that mean old sadist!") are excluded from consideration. Thus by assigning value to the two different modes of response, Kaplan portrays some kinds of art as being too "immature" to trigger imaginative response.

For popular art, the "reaction" by the audience is part of the single Act programmed by the popular artist using the work of art as Agency. But the aesthetic "response" to high art is a separate Act, part of a chain event wherein the work of art becomes the Agency by which a member of the audience achieves insight or personal growth. Detached from the initial Act of stimulation, this response achieves greater meaning for a philosopher who stresses individual growth and the development of a unique personality. For Kaplan, the formal conventions of popular art inhibit free will in terms of audience response, while the conventions of high art promote it. Later, in Chapter III, we shall see how well Kaplan's premises hold up.

Dramatism, Authorial Intention, And Artistic Conventions

The first question on authorship for a Dramatistic critic would be that which asks what *Act* is being performed when someone creates a work of fiction. Does an author write a book or screenplay to find self-fulfillment? Is he/she merely passing time, or desperately trying to escape the nine-to-five world? Is the audience given consideration at any point in the process? What possible variations are there in how artists view the role of the audience?

These questions all relate to the much-debated topic of *authorial intention*. The common view is that authorial intention encompasses the Act of investing a work with a determinate meaning that may be understood by an audience. The scope of this definition has come under serious questioning, however, by New Critics such as W.K. Wimsatt and Monroe Beardsley and by "newer" critics of all stamps, especially Deconstructionists.[9] The New Critics argue that a work of art can never mean exactly what an author may be thinking of, and that therefore meaning must be viewed as a function of the audience's response to the linguistic structures present in the text. The author must be written out of the scenario.

More recently, E.D. Hirsch, Jr., has argued for the existence of a "type idea" by which meaning may be shared by artist and audience alike.[10] The work of art, in Hirsch's model, serves as a scene or backdrop against which our consciousnesses project themselves. The act of creating art is the mirrored counterpart to the act of experiencing a work of art; the linguistic structures inherent in the work bring both artist and audience to the same type idea.

Hirsch's model is compatible with a Dramatistic view of authorship insofar as it recognizes that the creation of a work of art is a social Act. While it may be true that some works of art are designed for purely private purposes (auto-entertainment, therapy, etc.), they become social artifacts as soon as an audience comes into contact with them. And just as it is possible for us to use the medium of language to engage in discourse with ourselves, it is equally true that language is an Agency designed for a social Scene. If the Purpose of discourse is to convey the Agent's attitude toward something to someone else, then language by definition must be an efficacious tool. Since language must employ symbols to stand for objects and activities, the Agent-Agency ratio becomes critical when we consider authorial intention; how the author uses language and how he/she understands its limitations will determine how clearly meaning is conveyed.

A work of fiction is a more complex act of communication than a single command or promise. Fiction requires an understanding of a variety of elements—plot structures, character, the use of metaphor—before "type classification" may take place. Much more elaborate information is presented to us, and much less emphasis is placed on what we are to do with the information. Hirsch's notion of "shared type" can be likened to the concept of "convention," a concept which involves enlarging the scenic circumference within which linguistic communication takes place in order to give consideration to the additional resources brought in from the artist's and the audience's experience, resources involving both patterns of language use and patterns of life experience.

Insofar as they facilitate communication, conventions may be seen as agreed-upon structures which provide a context or Scene within which discourse may occur (and here I include both linguistic discourse and "discursive" or "message-containing" symbols in forms other than language, such as photography). As Steven Mailloux has defined them, conventions are "publicly-known and agreed-upon procedures for making intelligible the world, behavior, communication and literary texts. They are group-licensed strategies for constructing meaning, describable in terms of rules for intelligibility."[11] Mailloux distinguishes three types of conventions: traditional, prescriptive or regulative and constitutive. Traditional conventions are those that legitimize past regularities, e.g., standing up for the national anthem at a football game. Prescriptive conventions regulate future action, e.g., "Use a gun, go to prison." Constitutive conventions are descriptive rules assigning meaning, e.g., adherence to all felicity conventions pertaining to a speech act equals (or "counts as") a complete speech act. According to Mailloux, a general theory of interpretation would view all these conventions as constitutive in that they make meaning possible. A traditional convention such as standing for the national anthem is constitutive insofar as we adhere or fail to adhere to it: failure to stand *counts as* (constitutes) a lack of patriotism, disrespect for the flag, etc.

The phrase "counts as" in the previous sentence is significant in light of the Dramatistic model we have been developing. It is a recognition of the fact that every act of communication demands some sort of inner mental form that "stands in place of" or *counts as* some object or idea. We relate real-world objects and events analogically, creating meaning-structures by ordering them into familiar patterns. Kenneth Burke uses the term "patterns of experience" to refer to the most basic patterns that the human organism alembicates in the course of living in the natural and social world, by the adjustments we make in responding to a particular environment. As Burke notes:

> A particular environmental condition may be: a cruel father, an indulgent mother, a long stretch of poverty, the death of a favorite aunt, rough treatment at the hands of other boys, gentle years in a garden, what you will. Any such specific environmental condition calls forth and stresses certain of the universal experiences as being more relevant to it, with a slighting of those less relevant. Such selections are "patterns of experience." They distinguish us as "characters."[12]

Burke's model suggests the following description of how meaning is transmitted through art: 1) an artist who is a "character" in his own right by virtue of his pattern of experience, 2) creates a work of art that symbolically embeds a particular pattern of experience, a pattern which may be similar to the author's or very different from it, which in any case has been "filtered" through it, while 3) individual members of the audience experience the work of art and symbolically interpret the patterns in the work via their own "filters." The symbol may appeal to members of the audience for a variety of reasons: 1) the patterns of experience may be similar for artist and audience; 2) the formal properties of the work may be so expertly crafted that they present a "compelling" pattern for the audience; or 3) there may be "compensatory gains" in the appeal a different pattern has simply by virtue of being "different" (*Statement*, pp. 178-79).

Communicative perfection, to Burke, is impossible to achieve. "Perfection," as Burke views it, involves a complete identity of experience between artist and audience. Thus, "Perfection could exist only if the entire range of the reader's and writer's experience were identical down to the last detail. Universal and permanent perfection could exist only if this entire range of experiences were identical for all men forever" (*Statement*, p. 179). The aim of the poetic dialectic, then, is to strive toward perfection through the vicarious sharing of experience made possible through art.

At this juncture we begin to notice the tremendous challenge set before popular artists. Creating for a mass audience, the popular artist must anticipate and satisfy incredibly diverse patterns of experience. The heterogeneity of the audience makes it virtually impossible to create works of art which have symbolic appeal by virtue of close similarities in the patterns of experience undergone by both artist and audience. Indeed, as Gans has suggested, the popular artist is generally of a higher social class than his or her audience, and thus has little experience in common with them.[13] In contrast, the artist fashioning works for the "high" taste culture has a pattern of experience much more identical with that of his/her audience. As Gans notes, audience enjoyment of a work of high art often involves identification with the artist and the community of critics as much as it involves identification with the work itself.[14] Thus high art has a homogeneous elite which maintains a spirit of *communitas* uniting artists, critics and audiences. The popular artist, on the other hand, is most often an anonymous craftsman, fashioning works that have formulaic content and formal conventions as the basis of appeal. In general, we may conclude that popular works appeal to their audiences because they present expertly-crafted formal properties which match the genre expectations of the audience.

These formal properties of popular art are highly conventionalized, as we will discover in the next chapter. They are constitutive conventions inasmuch as they "count as" a set of guidebooks to the "real," everyday world. From the point of view of the audience, these guidebooks serve as an Agency to help make sense of the social, universe. Identification with "socially correct" procedures for dealing with certain typical situations (e.g., a "betrayed" wife in a soap opera has social approval for bitterly announcing her reasons for seeking a divorce) suggests means of responding to similar situations in real life. Just as we adopt the hairstyles of film stars, we adopt speech patterns and methods of overtly displaying our emotions. Popular art helps socialize its audiences into a common culture by providing a set of conventional responses which carry stock symbolic meaning. In Dramatistic terms, the Purpose of popular art within the Scene of the larger social structure is that it can function as a sort of "glue" uniting diverse peoples by providing conventional patterns of social behavior.

The popular artist may on occasion be someone who acts from within the same conventional structures as the audience and who creats intuitively, by combining conventional symbols in an appealing fashion. (The lyrics of country-and-western singer Hank Williams seem to have been written in this manner.) Alternately, the popular artist may be someone who can hold two views concurrently, on the one hand capturing and making use of social conventions and on the other examining the outer world as it may be encountered "purely," without appeal to stock responses. Insofar as the popular artist serves as the "voice of the people," he/she would tend to be the Hank Williams type, creating from within the conventional structures. But insofar as the artist serves the "classical" function described by British film critic Raymond

Durgnat of making the complicated world of flux and shadow more comprehensible to the general populace, he/she would tend to be more representative of the second model, that of the artist serving as a "bridge" between "pure" and "conventional" response.[15]

That such a bridge is necessary reflects an existential knot that I call the "Dialectician's Dilemma." The dilemma is that while we are individually capable of "pure," unconventional responses, we are unable to communicate them to others. They cannot be validated within a social context because no Scene can be provided as a referential backdrop. Only when symbolically transformed into conventional structures can my sense of the world be matched up against someone else's; a "pure," unfiltered act of communication is impossible.

In this light, consider the many works of popular art that are fashioned collaboratively, with no single artist being "in charge." Motion pictures, for example, are produced by a team of artists: directors, screenwriters, cinematographers, designers, editors, composers, choreographers, actors, and so on. The final product cannot be said to have been fashioned by any one individual, the claims of *auteur* criticism notwithstanding.[16] Even popular novels are often written by teams of writers and editors working from elaborate style sheets emphasizing basic do's and don'ts of plot and characterization.

Several questions immediately come to mind when one thinks of collaborative artistry in the popular arts. How does one go about defining the "intentional act"? How can a "unified vision" be presented under such circumstances? Are there "major" and "minor" contributors? What differences are there among different media? Where do we draw the line between a "gatekeeper" function (such as copy editing or designing a promotional campaign) and "artistry"?

Not all these questions can be answered in the present study, though they demand attention. Nor can we assert absolutely that "collective ethos" is a valid concept for one medium but not for another, or even that it should apply in all cases within the same medium. A case-by-case investigation of the creation of several works of art would probably reveal several patterns. One detective novel may be written by a single, original writer, while another may be produced as a spoof by a team of *New York Times* staff writers working collaboratively. What is clear is that there is a need for more critical attention to the way several artists work together to contribute to the final product. Traditional concepts of unity and purpose must be reviewed, and the Romantic assumptions underlying them must be modified in light of collaborative creation.

I would provisionally suggest that collective ethos involves a dialectic among various artists whereby individual attitudes toward the phenomenal world and toward the Purpose of the work get sorted out and merged into a unified "intentional Act" embodied within conventional structures appropriate for the particular symbolic message. A different sort of unity thus suggests itself to the critic dealing with collaboratively produced works of popular art. Instead of asking how well the individual author has woven the elements needed to make a good work of art, the critic may concentrate on how well various creators worked together to produce a harmoniously blended work. A Western film in which the hero maintains a stern, silent strength, as instructed by the director, and in which the camera is set by the cinematographer at a low angle to emphasize the height of the hero can be ruined by a capricious composer whose personal sense of the absurd leads him to use a comic ragtime piece for the showdown scene. Fortunately for the audience, film producers are generally motivated by dreams of box office revenues, and they seldom allow such contrapuntally clashing stuff to be released.

"Jaws": Collaborative Authorship In The Making Of The Movie

In the final section of this chapter I shall examine how the popular film version of *Jaws* was created, so as to illuminate the theory I have been expounding. In particular, I will use the

Dramatistic concept of Agent to shed light on the process whereb_· several artists worked in close collaboration to produce the final product. The same organizational plan is intended for the chapters on form and audience, first a discussion of theoretical concepts and problems raised by the Dramatistic method, and then examination of a sample work of recent popular art, with representation given to products of different media. Ultimately, I hope to demonstrate that some insightful practical criticism can result from an application of Dramatism to popular art, criticism that goes beyond the "objective" analysis of form and content and begins to explore the interrelationships among producers and consumers of popular art.

The history of *Jaws* reveals that from the very outset it was intended to be a "blockbuster," appealing to as wide an audience as possible. *Jaws* began its life as a film when producers Richard Zanuck and David Brown acquired the rights to Peter Benchley's novel in May 1973, eight months before the hardback book was nationally marketed. Film producers often have inside "leads" on major book projects undertaken by the large publishing houses, so it is not unusual for publishers to complete contracts for various subsidiary rights, including film rights, before releasing books they hope will become best-sellers. The additional revenue from these rights, plus the assurance that a novel stands a good chance of being released by a major film distributor, aid publishers in promoting new novels. In the case of *Jaws*, producers Brown and Zanuck helped market the novel by appearing on television and radio "talk shows," plugging both the book and film fully a year before the movie version was released.[17]

The conversion from novel to film required several writers and considerable input from the director, Steven Spielberg, and from several of the major stars. According to screenwriter Carl Gottlieb, who shared writers' billing with Peter Benchley, Benchley was paid approximately $250,000 for the rights to the novel and for a "first draft" screenplay that was altered considerably by Gottlieb and by veteran screenwriter Howard Sackler.[18] After Benchley had written about three drafts, in consultation with Spielberg, Sackler was asked to do a rewrite to deal with "some elements of the novel that seem to cry out for change, a subplot to be eliminated, and an overall filmic thrust yet to be developed" (*Log*, p. 48). Sackler's work was produced after four weeks of intensive effort in a Beverly Hills hotel room, though much of the dialogue and many of the major scenes used in the final film were written by Gottlieb after he was hired as a screenwriter on April 22, 1974.

By that date, some second-unit location shooting of great white sharks had already been completed in the South Pacific, a budget had been drawn up, some roles had been cast, locations had been scouted and tentative plans had been made for the filming schedule. These facts are important in demonstrating how *ad hoc* the production of a popular film can be, with many major creative decisions being made even as production efforts are fully underway. The Scene within which the film director's imagination may act is thus narrowed in scope, with possible plot lines being reduced in number.

In a situation like this, the dialectic is one of Agency-Agents, with the demand of the cinematic medium and the film business blurring the concept of authorial intention. A "grammar of motives" for the film version of *Jaws* would in many ways be more complex and less sharply defined than a study of Benchley's intentions in the novel. Thus, evaluations of quality aside, it is often more difficult to deal responsibly with popular art than with "high" art. That is to say, a work of popular art embodies all of the complex human motives that characterize "high" art, multiplied by the stresses of the marketplace and the fact that all these forces are at work with a number of Agents: screenwriters, directors, film editors and the like.

An interesting sidelight developed from Gottlieb's dual roles as screenwriter and actor, playing the part of the publisher of the town newspaper. The publisher's role had been more extensive in early drafts of the screenplay, but as Gottlieb writes:

> As the Writer, it was my sad duty to write myself out of the

picture as superfluous, and as an Actor, my heart bled with every cut. Talk about ego splits—you haven't experienced schizophrenia until you sit in a story conference discussing whether your presence in a scene is necessary or desirable, knowing that every cut you make as a writer destroys you as an actor, and that every objection you raise has to be judged on two levels: the writer's defense of a character in a scene, and the actor's dismay at being eliminated from a juicy role. (*Log*, pp. 65-66.)

The Dramatist would view this dilemma with tremendous interest. Gottlieb had to consider his vision of the unity of his artistic creation and its effect on audiences while struggling with a desire to maximize his own private gain as a performer. Purpose shifted as the Agent found himself reflecting on the question: Which Act should I perform, in what guise, and in which Scene?

The transformation of the character of Matt Hooper, the young ichthyologist, as the novel was converted to film is another instance where the collaborative efforts of several artists can be seen. In Benchley's novel, Hooper is an "outsider" who figures prominently in a subplot dealing with his affair with Sheriff Brody's wife. In the film, Hooper is one of a trio of heroes (the other two being the Sheriff and the grizzled old seaman, Quint), the one "who represents civilization and education and modern science" (*Log*, p. 70). Earlier drafts had already eliminated the sexual subplot, but when Richard Dreyfuss was cast as Hooper in late April 1974, he had several objections to the way in which his character had been developed. In a three-way conference with Gottlieb and Spielberg that took place in a Boston hotel room, Dreyfuss offered several ideas designed to enhance Hooper's personality, including the comic scene in which Dreyfuss, as Hooper, crunches a styrofoam cup in mocking response to Quint's (Robert Shaw) ostentatious crushing of a metal beer can (*Log*, pp. 74-75). The calculus of "multiple Agents" is thus further complicated in a medium such as film, where even the Actor playing a role can become an Agent or "author" making major contributions to the final product.

Some minor changes in the original conception of the film

came about by sheer accident. The original version of a scene wherein the Sheriff and Hooper discover a silent, floating boat and get scared out of their wits after Hooper dives and discovers the severed, shark-gnawed head of a local resident, had been written to include Meadows (Gottlieb), the publisher. The original scene was filmed during the daytime, and during the shooting, Gottlieb accidentally fell overboard, spoiling the footage. After some discussion with director Spielberg, it was decided that the scene would play better if Meadows were cut from the scene and if it were to occur at night, with a suitably eerie atmosphere building up suspense (*Log,* pp. 102-107).

Jaws differs from most films in terms of its production history for two major reasons: 1) the principal screenwriter, Gottlieb, was working on scenes used in the final production even while shooting was underway in Martha's Vineyard, and 2) the film's editor, Verna Fields, was present with the rest of the company on location, assembling sequences from the daily "rushes" even as the film was being shot. Both Gottlieb and Fields were in close, daily contact with Spielberg (Gottlieb even shared the same rented house), so that a "triumvirate" of top collaborators can be said to be primarily responsible for the final shape of the film. In most film productions, a shooting script is in final form, except for minor, on-the-spot dialogue changes, before location shooting begins, in order to give set designers, costumers, property managers, cinematographers and other support personnel plenty of time to work out the logistics for each day's shooting. With *Jaws* it seemed to the support crew as if things were being "made up" as shooting went along (*Log,* p. 99). It is also customary for the film editor to start work only *after* all location and studio shooting has taken place. But Verna Fields, according to Gottlieb, "is one of those who insists, if it's at all possible, on being present for the entire filming of a picture, on location or at home, and working in close collaboration with the director" (*Log,* p. 134). Spielberg had previously worked with Fields on *The Sugarland Express* and found this sort of close collaboration very helpful. Burke would view this mode of creation as being well-suited to the development of a dialectically unified vision against the challenging Scene of location shooting, since both director and editor are exposed to the same day-to-day variables that may alter the final product. Essentially, a Scene-Agent ratio exists, bringing about a set of common experiences on location that can be referred to at the time of cutting room conferences. Without such common experience, the director and editor may find themselves at odds because the director may be drawing on "background" impressions that would be difficult to communicate to an editor who had not been physically present.

Thematically, the film is designed to grip the audience on two levels. It is a straightforward "monster/adventure yarn with overtones of social conscience and individual action for the common good throughout" (*Log*, p. 68). As we have seen, the sexual subplot in the novel was consciously eliminated in order to present a more direct tale of man against shark. In addition, the artists shaping the film develop the characters of Quint, Hooper and Brody differently in the film than the same characters appear in the novel; the film stresses their contrasting personalities in order to present more fully a unique conception of the American hero as someone who can recover from guilt and error to achieve ultimate victory. This was a theme much on the minds of American audiences in 1974-75, the period immediately following Watergate, suggesting that perhaps one consideration in the minds of the Agents who fashioned these changes from the novel was an awareness that a bolder statement of the character differences would appeal more strongly to an audience looking for a new definition of hero.

Quint, played by Robert Shaw, is a rugged old commercial fisherman and captain of a charter boat who lives alone in a worn wooden structure on the water's edge, decorated with scores of sharks' jaws. He is grizzled and tough-talking, a variant on the individualistic male hero type associated with John Wayne. Two factors are stressed: 1) he is a traditional male chauvinist, raising a toast to "swimmin' wi' bow-legged wimmen" and making fun of Sheriff Brody's wife when she expresses concern for her husband's safety, and 2) he is a "walking ghost," a hero model out of step with the modern age.

The latter point is established in a scene aboard Quint's boat, the *Orca*, when he tells Hooper and Brody how he survived the sinking of a Navy ship delivering atomic weapons in World War II, a disaster claiming the lives of most of his fellow sailors, who were eaten by sharks. This scene establishes Quint's ultimate fate of being killed by the shark by qualitatively paralleling the story of Ahab losing his leg in *Moby Dick*. The artists know that the audience is familiar with Ahab's story and his fate, and thus they prepare the audience to accept Quint's eventual doom. The Agents are quite aware that an audience can be easily sidetracked, worrying about Quint's death. Since their main point lies in offering various hero models up to the audience for comparison, the artists use the *Moby Dick* parallel to foreshadow Quint's doom. With the question of Quint's fate having become unimportant in terms of dramatic development and the building of suspense, the audience is free to assess the appropriateness of his fate in comparison with that of the other characters being offered as potential hero models. The audience has "room to think" and judges that clearly Quint's macho methods are inefficacious in solving the complex problems of the modern world. One message offered by *Jaws* is that the iconoclast as hero is dead.

Hooper symbolizes the danger of placing too much reliance on technology. A Sputnik generation hero, Hooper represents the ultimate technophile, continually spouting out precise, scientific terms for every type of shark known to humankind, as if this were a way to ward off the menace. To a generation nurtured on *Mister Wizard* and *Star Trek*, Hooper is fascinating, because he has all the fancy gadgets that whirl and flash and go bleep. Yet he lives under a grand illusion. He imagines that he can somehow protect himself from the monster by surrounding himself with expensive scientific equipment. His gadgets, however, become a symbolic device whereby the artists "bait" the audience into identifying with Hooper and then "switch" their feelings by showing how technology fails to protect him when the real battle with the shark is at hand. The pivotal scene occurs when Hooper enters his "invulnerable" shark cage, only to have it battered to pieces by the force of the monster. Hooper manages to survive, but he remains trapped underwater while the main battle takes place overhead. He symbolizes the kind of person who gets so wrapped up in material possessions that he loses all sight of moral conflict. The didactic message of the artists is again established: faith in technology will not substitute for genuine heroism.

With Quint dead and Hooper trapped underwater, only Sheriff Brody remains to do battle with the shark. Like a Horatio Alger character, he combines pluck and luck to singlehandedly defeat the monster, stuffing an air cannister into its maw and blowing it up with a well-placed bullet. The audience cheers Brody's victory, identifying with him as a hero who has overcome his own fear and his own past errors to achieve ultimate victory. Brody's initial guilt over bowing to local real estate interests who influenced him not to close the beaches in response to the first shark attack ultimately is transformed into a resolve to defeat the beast that has brought him to an awareness of his own capacity for corruption.

In this section, I have dealt with some aspects of the production history of *Jaws* as they relate to the working relationship of the major Agents who "authored" the film, and I have shown how the conscious reworking of the major characters by these Agents serves to accentuate a didactic statement to the audience concerning the nature of heroism. The Pentad serves as an aid in both processes, but especially in the latter. "Objective" criticism, which would look at the formal characteristics of the film as they stand alone from artists and audience, and "reader response" criticism, as it would view the activities of the audience, would both fall short of the insights revealed by the Dramatistic model. The reader response critic, for example, would show how the reader "comes to an awareness" that Brody is a more acceptable hero than Quint or Hooper. The Dramatist, on the other hand, expands the Circumference of the discussion and allows for the Act of creation to stand alongside the Act of response. Artists can thus be seen as "persuaders" who consciously manipulate their audiences into adopting a particular point of view by the way they ramify a particular symbol.

We see this manipulation occurring in *Jaws* as the question, "What qualities should a modern American hero have?" is forced to the front. Quint and Hooper serve as foils, and are eliminated by artistic technique. Quint is alienated from the other characters by his gruffness and his antipathy toward women. He is alienated further from the audience by his association with Captain Ahab. Hooper's alienation contains a twist, a twist which forces members of the audience to reflect upon their own blind love for material possessions. The artists instill a didactic message as they knowingly "distance" the audience from Hooper by robbing him of the opportunity for heroism and the audience of a chance to see the person who promotes love of material objects prove victorious. We need to keep this didacticism in mind as we reflect upon Abraham Kaplan's assertion that popular art creates only "reactions" not "responses." Kaplan's assumptions about audience passivity will be discussed further in Chapter III, but for now we may note that popular *artists* do not always simply fall into the trap of reinforcing conventional values.

To summarize, in *Jaws* we find that a group of close collaborators has worked its stamp on a popular adventure yarn, refashioning the major characters via a dialectic involving several writers, an aggressive director and film editor, and insightful actors, so that the end result is an "intentional Act" designed to present a new model of a "fallible" hero to an audience suffering from a common belief that heroism is dead and that Watergate-style corruption is the fated concomitant of leadership. Burke's emphasis on the artist as communicator has led us to examine how the artists' awareness of audience expectations results in conscious craftsmanship in developing the principal characters. The saga of how the film came to be made shows how several collaborators were brought together and how they grew to develop a unified vision of the film as they worked closely together in Martha's Vineyard. It is in allowing for a consideration of this Scene-Agent ratio—the impact of the working environment upon the artists—that Dramatism differs most from other forms of criticism. Dramatism thus opens up a wider range of possibilities in the sources of information that can be used by critics and researchers. Such relatively unexplored tools as writers' diaries, trade magazine interviews with film-makers on location, studio memoranda and the like may prove to be of considerable use as future researchers document more thoroughly the decisions made by popular artists as they engage in their craft.

Notes

[1] Kenneth Burke, *Language as Symbolic Action: Essays on Life, Literature, and Method* (Berkeley: Univ. of California Press, 1966), p. 16. Hereinafter referred to as *Language*; subsequent reference citations will appear in parentheses in the text.

[2] Kenneth Burke, *A Grammar of Motives* (New York: Prentice-Hall, 1945), p. 318. Hereinafter referred to as *Grammar*; subsequent reference citations will appear in parentheses in text.

[3] Kenneth Burke, "Dramatism," *International Encyclopedia of the Social Sciences*, ed. David L. Still (New York: Macmillan, and The Free Press, 1968), Vol. VII, p. 445.

[4] Michael George Feehan, "A Dramatistic Grammar of Literary Reception: Perspectives on 'Leaves of Grass'," Diss. Univ. of Southern California, 1979, p. 55.

[5] Feehan, p. 59.

[6] See Edward Shils, "Mass Society and Its Culture," *Daedalus*, 89 (1960), 289-90.

[7] Herbert J. Gans, *Popular Culture and High Culture: An Analysis and Evaluation of Taste* (New York: Basic Books, 1974).

[8] Abraham Kaplan, "The Aesthetics of the Popular Arts," in *Modern Culture and the Arts*, Ed. James B. Hall and Barry Ulanov, 2nd ed. (New York: McGraw-Hill, 1967).

[9] William K. Wimsatt, Jr., and Monroe Beardsley, "The Intentional Fallacy," in *The Verbal Icon: Studies in the Meaning of Poetry* (Lexington: Univ. of Kentucky Press, 1954).

[10] E.D.Hirsch, Jr., *Validity in Interpretation* (New Haven: Yale Univ. Press, 1967).

[11] Steven John Mailloux, "Interpretive Conventions and Recent Anglo-American Literary Theory," Diss. Univ. of Southern California, 1978, p. 123.

[12] Kenneth Burke, *Counter-Statement* (1931; rpt. Berkeley: Univ. of California Press, 1968), p. 150-51. Hereinafter referred to as *Statement*; subsequent reference citations will appear in parentheses in text.

[13] Gans, p. 24.

[14] Gans, pp. 75-79.

[15] See Raymond Durgnat, "Art and Audience," *British Journal of Aesthetics*, 10 (1970). Durgnat essentially argues that current criticism is oriented toward the "Romantic" motives of the high culture artist who creates for self-expression, and that it ignores the "Classical" social role of the popular artist. This notion will be taken up again in Chapter III.

[16] My own view is that *auteur* criticism represents the desires of "elite" critics functioning within a set of Romantic suppositions about the nature of artistry and hoping to legitimize film as a high culture art form. The magnificent creative consciousness of the director-*auteur* is highlighted in emulation of the schools of literary criticism which focus on individual writers, their belief systems, and their stylistic innovations.

[17] John Getze, "Jaws Swims to the Top in Ocean of Publicity," *Los Angeles Times*, 28 Sept. 1975, Part 7, pp. 1-2.

[18] Carl Gottlieb, *The Jaws Log* (New York: Dell, 1975), see esp. pp. 19, 48, and 152. Hereinafter referred to as *Log*; subsequent reference citations will appear in parentheses in the text.

II
Form in Popular Art

Most contemporary popular art critics are familiar with John G. Cawelti's work on popular formulae. In a number of books and articles published in recent years, Cawelti has put forth a convincing case for the notion that popular art works are enjoyed by mass audiences because they articulate conventional themes within the bounds of formulaic structures appealing to our basic social and psychological makeup.[1] Cawelti argues that the "dialectic of cultural and artistic interests" at a given moment in history can be studied in order to shed light on the major social, political, and psychological concerns of an age as revealed through its popular art.[2] At the same time, one can come to understand how art is appreciated by observing how it reflects the concerns of its times. Thus Cawelti justifies the study of formal qualities of popular art by demonstrating how much can be revealed about social history and human psychology by such studies.

Kenneth Burke, on the other hand, is a name virtually unknown to the average student of the popular arts. This is unfortunate, for not only is Burke's work on the nature of form prior to Cawelti's, and for the most part compatible with it, but it is also much more comprehensive. Burke's concept of form can be applied to a work of art viewed *extrinsically*, as it relates to the wider social context out of which it emerges, as well as *intrinsically*, in terms of the formal structures inherent in the work itself. It provides for an analysis of the contribution of the artist and for the interplay between the work and its audience. Before we return to Cawelti, therefore, we will take a longer look at Burke's concept of form.

Kenneth Burke and Form

Most of Burke's major ideas on form can be found in *Counter-Statement*, published in 1931, before a full-blown theory of Dramatism had been developed. But like all Burke's writings, *Counter-Statement* is part of a natural progression of consistent ideas. As a consequence, one who looks back at *Counter-Statement* from the perspective furnished by the later writings would have no trouble melding the concept of form stated in 1931 with the theory of Dramatism developed in the *Grammar* and the *Rhetoric*.

Burke defines form as "the creation of an appetite in the mind of the auditor, and the adequate satisfying of that appetite" (*Statement*, p. 31). This view is harmonious with the assumption that art is a part of life experience, not an element that can be separated from the other components of human existence. In Burke's view, "Art, at least in the great periods when it has flowered, was the conversion or transcendence of emotion into eloquence, and was thus a factor added to life" (*Statement*, p. 41). Formal conventions occupy a role critically intertwined with human experience. Burke sees form as a tool that helps us symbolize our inner feelings. Form has *cause* (the human desire to externally express inner feelings) and *Purpose* (as an aid in persuading us of the "human-ness" of our works of art). From a rhetorical standpoint, form is the "glue" that unites artist and audience.

In a chapter on "The Psychology of Form" in *Counter-Statement*, Burke distinguishes between a psychology of information and a psychology of form. In the former, the human appetite for data is satisfied. The reader of *Moby Dick*, for example, is given a considerable amount of information about the methods of whale hunting used in nineteenth-century New England. Elements related to plot (*what* occurs in a work of art rather than *how* it occurs) are tied to the psychology of information. According to Burke, audience interest is maintained most appropriately when devices of *surprise* and *suspense* are used. As Burke defines it, "Suspense is the concern over the possible outcome of some specific detail of plot rather than for general qualities. Thus, 'Will A marry B or C?, is suspense" (*Statement*, p. 38).

In instances where the psychology of information is predominant in a work of art to the virtual exclusion of the psychology of form, the audience is left with only a partial sense of satisfaction. Devoid of symbolically ramified analogs to human emotion, or to what Burke terms "racial appetites," such works give no pleasure in rereading. If the audience has been made to hunger for information alone, and if the appetite has been satisfied, then even with the tools of surprise and suspense the excitement is gone the second time around. An aesthetically impoverished Whodunit loses its impact as soon as the audience knows the name of the murderer. An aesthetically rich Whodunit, on the other hand, may be read over and over again, for it offers insight into the depths of human motivation. Only that *eloquence* which characterizes the psychology of form and which stimulates an approving "Yes, this *is* the way of the human soul!" can maintain interest again and again. As Burke puts it:

> Truth in art is not the discovery of facts, not an addition to human knowledge in the scientific sense of the word. It is, rather, the exercise of human propriety, the formulation of symbols which rigidify our sense of poise and rhythm. Artistic truth is the externalization of taste. (*Statement*, p. 42.)

If form is a set of analogs to inner states of being (Burke mentions both the "concrete" functions such as the rhythm of the human heartbeat and the "ineffable" ones such as love, guilt, sorrow, etc.), then the task of the critical theorist must be to demonstrate how these analogs actually are developed in works of art involving different media of communication. This Burke attempts to do in the longest section of *Counter-Statement*, the "Lexicon Rhetoricae." In the "Lexicon," Burke describes five aspects of form: 1) syllogistic progression, 2) qualitative progression, 3) repetitive form, 4) conventional form, and 5) minor or incidental forms. We will take up each in its turn.

Syllogistic progression, Burke writes, "is the form of a perfectly conducted argument, advancing step by step" (*Statement*, p. 124). Thus a story of ratiocination by Poe, wherein a detective sifts through clues and eliminates possible suspects one by one, tracking a culprit down in a methodical manner, is an example of syllogistic progression. Typically this aspect of form applies to our understanding of the motives underlying a character's actions. We may enjoy the final acting-out of revenge, for instance, because our appetite has been stimulated by the acts of malice perpetrated against the protagonist. We *identify* with the situation the hero has found himself in and we share in his experience as he grows in his desire for vengeance, step by step, as the plot unfolds.

Qualitative progression relies not upon the logical interconnectedness of the *incidents* in the plot, as with syllogistic progression, but rather the interconnectedness of the "quality" of certain scenes. Perhaps the best example of qualitative progression is the "comic relief" scene which frequently follows a scene of high tension or violence. The comic relief allows us to briefly relax and gain some perspective and distance on what we have just experienced. Burke notes that unlike a syllogistic progression, which usually occurs in such an orderly manner that we come to *expect* the next incident, a qualitative progression first happens, and then we "recognize its rightness after the incident." Qualitative progressions are well-crafted if they enable us to be "put into a state of mind which another state of mind can appropriately follow" (*Statement*, p. 125).

Repetitive form, according to Burke, is the "consistent maintaining of a principle under new guises" (*Statement,* p. 125). This aspect of form can be articulated in many ways. Burke offers the example of Swift enumerating many details to illustrate the discrepancy in size between Gulliver and the Lilliputians. Each detail reinforces the main theme. Another way in which repetitive form may be present is in the "clustering" of images appropriate to a particular theme or topic, a succession of nature images to amplify a lyric poem on Spring, for example. Repetitive form, Burke argues, is basic to any work of art, or to any act of human communication.It is necessary in order for us to be oriented properly to a particular topic, or as Burke puts it, "it is our only method of 'talking on the subject' " (*Statement*, p. 125).

Conventional form relies upon the element of "categorical expectancy" (Burke's term) among members of the audience. The presence of the chorus in a Greek play, for example, is anticipated by one who is about to witness a Greek tragedy; it is a convention of the genre. Similarly, the fact that a sonnet contains fourteen lines or that a limerick has an *aabba* rhyme scheme are further instances of conventional form. Like the English common law tradition, it may be exceedingly difficult to trace the source of many conventions, and all the bother involved may not tell us anything of significance. Suffice it to say that certain structures become associated with certain themes or certain modes of presentation or certain moods, and that these structures are widely understood by artists and audiences, both giving assent to the "appropriateness" of the structure for the particular work of art. In general, Burke's concept of conventional form is compatible with Cawelti's theory of popular formula, about which we will have more to say in the next section.

Finally, we have minor or incidental forms. These are the elements of style—metaphor, apostrophe, chiasmus, etc.— which occur in great number in any work of art. Minor forms may be dissected from the whole and treated as aspects of the work unique unto themselves, but they serve a greater general purpose when they are studied in terms of their contribution to the unfolding of the work as a whole. Ahab's wooden leg, for instance, becomes important as a synecdochic representation of the complete man, with all his hurt and obsession.

Following this enumeration of the major aspects of form, Burke addresses two key questions: 1) Why do these forms have appeal? and 2) By what standard are they to be judged as "correct"? In responding to the first question, Burke asserts that formal structures in art are not unique. They are simply analogous to the structures by which the human mind reasons: He writes:

> There are formal patterns which distinguish our
> experience. They apply in art, since they apply outside of
> art.... We establish a direction by co-ordinates; we
> establish a curve by three points, and thereupon can to
> place other points that they will be intercepted by this curve.
> Thus, though forms need not be prior to experience, they are
> certainly prior to the work of art exemplifying them.
> (*Statement*, p. 141)

Even the minor forms such as contrast, comparison, metaphor,
series, chiasmus, and bathos are "implicit in the processes of
abstraction and generalization by which we think." In sum,
Burke asserts that "the formal aspects of art appeal in that
they exercise formal potentialities of the reader. They enable
the mind to follow processes amenable to it" (*Statement,* pp.
142-43).

The second question is really the essential question for all
criticism. Any critic who presumes to be able to assess a form
as "correct" or "incorrect" for a work of art must be able to state
the grounds by which he or she arrives at such judgments. For
Burke, the "correctness" or appropriateness of a given form for
a given work of art must be ascertained dialectically. A mere
intrinsic study of the formal properties of the work will not
suffice. The critic must examine the entire continuum of
communication, from artistry to audience response. A general
Burkean principle is that "Form, having to do with the creation
and gratification of needs, is 'correct' in so far as it gratifies the
needs which it creates" (*Statement*, p. 138). The "needs" are
needs of the audience. The dialectic is the interplay between a
work of art, presenting a powerful symbol of human emotion,
made eloquent by the vehicle of various aspects of form, and
the members of the audience, drawn into the work by formal
properties that parallel, as best as possible within the confines
of a given medium, the paradigms of "lived experience" that
accompany human emotion. A form is judged to be correct if it
satisfies all the "categorical expectancies" which it sets up and
if it avoids setting up expectations that run against the grain of
the symbol.

Dramatistically, a form which has appeal is one which

"works" within two "Scenes." The first is the intrinsic context of the work. Within the conventional form of the Gene Autry Western, for example, the hero is always kind to animals. For Autry to kick a dog would be a violation of the conventions intrinsic to the work, even though dog-kicking may be a "natural" act in the "outer" world. In addition, there is the Scene of the lived world. This Scene may encompass activities as subliminal as the workings of the autonomic nervous system or as overt and broadbased as our common pool of knowledge about the political structure of the United States. Thus we assent to the appropriateness of Dagwood Bumstead acting nervous and timid when approaching Mr. Dithers for a raise, because we can picture ourselves in a similar situation.

Form thus can be seen as the vehicle by which "patterns of experience" are symbolized and transmitted from artist to audience (see Chapter I). As Burke defines it, a symbol is a "verbal parallel to a pattern of experience" (*Statement*, p. 152). He offers the example of the self-pitying poet who feels his work has been undeservedly neglected, and who translates his own experience into a plot, "The King and the Peasant," about a kingly peasant and a shallow-minded king. Burke does not suggest that all works of art are simply embellishments of a given artist's own pattern of experience; he simply observes that such can be the case.

The symbol is easiest to transmit when the artist's pattern of experience is close to the audience's. But a symbol can have appeal for an audience even when the pattern it represents is new or strange. It can clarify situations which have hitherto been complex and ambiguous. It can touch on patterns that have been submerged (e.g., symbols of cruelty or incest). It can serve as a corrective to value conflicts. It can stimulate hidden desires, or provide vicarious escape from the tedium of everyday life. Other modes of appeal may be added to this list, but in general we may note that the patterns of experience lodged in a particular symbol do not necessarily need to be part of the *actual* experience of the artist or audience.

The artist uses various aspects of form to explore the ramifications of a particular symbol. For example, in order to make "The King and the Peasant" a believable story, there may have to be minor characters, quirks of personality, appropriate setting and other details to "flesh out" the characters. If the drama is written in a mimetic mode, there may even be a few minor contradictions. The "noble" peasant may have to have a few bad, peasant-like qualities such as roughness of speech. As a symbol is ramified by the formal structures present in a work of art, it more thoroughly articulates a particular pattern of experience. Thus the symbol is generative in the sense that it suggests the structure and course that the work of art will follow. Stated in terms of the Pentad, Purpose (as represented by the symbol) helps shape Scene (the structure of the work).

Burke and Cawelti

We are now ready to return to Cawelti, in particular to some of the ideas presented in *Adventure, Mystery, and Romance: Formula Stories as Art and Popular Culture*. In this recent volume, Cawelti adds flesh to earlier essays and articles, more fully elaborating his concepts of popular formula. In particular, Cawelti builds upon his earlier general definition of formula by analyzing the structures and the modes of appeal of various types of literary formulae, e.g., the detective story, the romance, the social melodrama, etc. Since he defines formula as "a combination or synthesis of a number of specific cultural conventions with a more universal story form or archetype," we can expect that Cawelti would make observations about both the basic psychological appeal of a particular story form and the specific appeal the form has within a narrower cultural context (*Adventure*, p. 6). For example, in discussing the Western, Cawelti notes that it has general roots in the adventure archetype and specific roots in the symbol of the American West as a place where the hero is bound to be caught up in the conflict between civilization and wilderness (*Adventure*, Chapter 8).

My general intent is not to spend a great deal of time on Cawelti's theories, but rather to demonstrate how his criticism as it is practiced is compatible with Dramatism and Burke's concept of for.n. There are three essential similarities between Cawelti and Burke: 1) both start from the premise that the interact on between the audience and the work is dialectical, not merely a behaviorist response to the formal "stimulus" of the work of art; 2) both place great emphasis on the artist's and audience's social environment as a "Scenic" backdrop for the work; and 3) both stress the prominence of the symbol as it is developed and carried forth by the formal properties of the work. Cawelti's position is staked out most clearly in his 1974 article "Myth, Symbol, and Formula," where he asserts that his approach to popular culture departs from traditional social and psychological determinism because "it rejects the concept of a single fundamental social or psychological dynamic in favor of viewing the appeal of a conventional literary pattern as the bringing into play of a variety of cultural, artistic, and psychological interests."[3] Here we see quite clearly that Cawelti is an antibehaviorist who views art as belonging to the world of Action, not mere Motion. Cawelti's basic orientation— here stressing the audience's rather than the artist's perspective—is similar to Burke's viewing art as a set of "strategies for situations."

In *Adventure, Mystery, and Romance*, we find that Cawelti views the social melodrama as perhaps the most complex popular formula because it is not as rigidly constructed as other forms (the Western, the hard-boiled detective story, etc.), but rather is a complex mixture of formulae that have evolved over time. As Cawelti defines the social melodrama:

> The structural characteristics of this formulaic type involve an interweaving of the patterns of melodrama with a particular set of current events or social institutions, the result being a complex double effect: the social setting is often treated rather critically with a good deal of anatomizing the hidden motives, secret corruption, and human folly underlying certain events or institutions; yet the main plot works out in proper melodramatic fashion to affirm, after appropriate tribulations and sufferings, that God is in his heaven and all's right with the world. The

> sympathetic and the good undergo much testing and difficulty, but are ultimately saved. (*Adventure,* p. 261)

One formal necessity of the social melodrama is that the writer's voice must appear to be that of an "authority" who "tries to make us feel that we have penetrated what shows on the surface to the inside story; he offers what appears to be the dust beneath the rug, the secret power behind the scenes" (*Adventure,* p. 262). Structurally, this necessitates the use of devices offering surprise and suspense, since the conventional social Scene must be "peeled away" to reveal the underlying Scene-behind-the-Scene. Combined with the hallmark of melodrama, the presentation of various trials and tribulations that the good characters must undergo, and of the machinations and ultimate punishment of the wicked, this means that the overall structure of the social melodrama must rely heavily on *individual episodes* supported by some larger organizing principle.

The type of organizing principle that an individual author typically uses will influence the formal arrangement of these episodes. For example, Cawelti notes that Harold Robbins "tends to write stories of the failure of success. His central characters pursue the phantoms of wealth and power only to discover that true fulfillment can only come through love, loyalty, and compassion" (*Adventure,* p. 280). The Robbins plot thus follows a protagonist through a syllogistic progression of episodes; the reader identifies with the symbol of the power-hungry hero whose jaded experiences only reinforce conventional concepts of goodness. The necessity for scenes of evil and corruption makes it easier for Robbins to use implausible coincidence and exaggerated spectacle to heighten the melodrama.

Burke and Cawelti are closest in their analyses in treating art as a *social artifact* emerging from a set of attitudes toward the larger social Scene, attitudes which may be explicitly understood and exploited by the artist or implicitly present in the work. Thus both men focus on how an author may use the audience's social knowledge to achieve certain dramatic effects. In analyzing the social melodrama, for example, Cawelti comes close to Burke's concept of qualitative progression in noting how Robbins strings together episodes of sexual experimentation and "perversity" as his protagonists undergo a sort of *Walpurgisnacht* on the road to eventually being satisfied with monogamistic love. If the underlying social attitude of mid-twentieth-century Americans did not favor a monogamistic ideal, Cawelti observes, then Robbins and other writers would not be able to secure agreement from their audiences as they construct works which qualitatively move toward this ideal by artistically arranging episodes of shocking contrast and harsh discord.

Indeed, as Cawelti traces the history of the social melodrama, he notes that best-selling works in this genre are more short-lived than most best-sellers in other popular formulae (note the lasting impact of Sir Arthur Conan Doyle's Sherlock Holmes detective stories, for instance, as opposed to Mrs. E.D.E.N. Southworth's social melodramas of roughly the same period). This failure of the social melodrama to have a lasting power on audiences, Cawelti feels, is primarily due to rapid changes in social values. The promulgation of "outworn" social values (e.g., the belief in a traditional Christian God as the only mark of goodness) is a hallmark of even fairly recent social melodramas. Unlike other forms, where archaic values can be tolerated because they are not instrumental in advancing the plot or in sorting out the "good guys" from the bad, the social melodrama depends upon the audience adhering to these values in order to gain assent to the appropriateness of the denouement.

For the serious student of the popular arts, then, Burke and Cawelti provide a thorough base for understanding the formal properties of popular art. As we have seen by examining Cawelti's analysis of one popular genre, the social melodrama, he provides a thoroughgoing examination of the modes of appeal of popular formulae, working out in considerable detail how symbols are generated and ramified through the conventions of these formulae. Burke is more the pure theorist and less the practical critic, but his Dramatistic method offers three major concepts which can be used in dissecting the formal aspects of any type of art. First is the Pentad, which allows us to examine both authorial intention and audience response.[4] Secondly, we have the concepts of identification and patterns of experience, which provide the links between the incidents in a fictional story and the Scenic backdrop of everyday life. Finally, we have the specific types of form as outlined in the "Lexicon Rhetoricae." Added together, these methodological tools allow us to better penetrate the mysteries of form in the popular arts.

Form and Television

As the newest and most powerful of the electronic media, television is seen by many critics as something too close to our daily experience for proper analysis. Most television criticism, therefore, is of the garden variety that appears in the daily newspapers or the FCC "social scientific" approach, which makes use of statistics on behavioral responses to Roadrunner cartoons as an aid to formulating policy on television violence. Few critics wander into the complicated area of television as a medium that contains unique formal properties which distinguish its content from that of traditional art forms.

One exception to this rule is Horace Newcomb, a student of Cawelti's who has applied Cawelti's notions concerning popular formulae to the medium of television. In *TV: The Most Popular Art,* Newcomb sets out to explore the ways "in which television changes and modifies traditional formulas, how it begins to create a sense of the 'television formula' with its own cultural significance."[5] In dealing with the Western formula as it has been modified by television, for example, Newcomb notes the diminution of the importance of outdoor scenery (awesome on the big screen in movie theaters but awkward in appearance on the small screen of TV) and the importance of continuing characters in such long-running television Westerns as *Gunsmoke* and *Bonanza*. The constraint imposed by a week-to-week series format means that the traditional syllogistic form of the Western film or novel, wherein a single action is developed and drawn to closure, is impossible to maintain. Instead, the continuing characters must be "without memory" in order to confront a new problem situation each week. As Newcomb notes:

> In this circular framework the classic issues of western adventure would have played themselves out long ago. In order to avoid this the producers have applied the western vision to a host of other problems. The problem-solution paradigm of the sitcom and the family focus of the domestic comedy have been combined with the Western formula in the creation of a new form of popular art.[6]

In this example, we see how Newcomb builds upon Cawelti's general theory of formulae by demonstrating how the constraints imposed by a particular medium will inevitably lead to some sort of modification of the formula. A more general statement of this view would be to say, for example, that a detective *novel* will be different in its formulaic aspects from a detective *film*, and so on.

In *TV: The Most Popular Art,* Newcomb suggests three components of an overall television aesthetic: intimacy, continuity, and history. By intimacy, Newcomb means both the closeness of the situation within which members of the audience experience material presented on television and the fact that interior scenes and face-to-face conversations are more appropriate to the small screen than they are to the wide screen in the movie theater. By continuity, Newcomb refers to the regular appearance of characters and standard sets (e.g., Archie Bunker's armchair) that form a comfortable and familiar environment for those of us watching regularly scheduled series. In probing aspects of continuity, Newcomb comes to the thought-provoking conclusion that:

> The real relationship with other media lies not in movies or
> radio, but in the novel. Television, like the literary form, can
> offer a far greater sense of density. Details take on an
> importance slowly, and within repeated patterns of action,
> rather than with the immediacy of other visual forms.[7]

Newcomb notes that television, like the novel, offers us a dense,
rich world "fully created by the artist." Finally, by history,
Newcomb means that television has become a medium where
contemporary issues are examined within unique formulaic
structures and where much of the time, they are removed to a
"mythical" historical time, where values can be more firmly
and concretely dealt with, as in the case of the television
Western, where contemporary topics such as racial prejudice
can be treated within the dramatic form of a Chinese worker
passing through Virginia City, Nevada, in the late nineteenth-
century era of *Bonanza*.

In focusing upon the formal properties which are brought
out by the nature of a medium such as television, and by the
nature of the audience's interaction with content as conveyed
by the medium, Newcomb is staking out a position which
stresses the role of the medium in a much more integrated
fashion than McLuhan, who has an almost "transcendental"
obsession with it. As we have noted earlier, the theory of
popular formulae as advanced by Cawelti and enhanced, in
this instance, by Newcomb is closely related to what Burke
means by the term "conventional form" (or "categorical
expectation"). In *Counter-Statement*, Burke discusses how
conventional form may evolve within a single medium over a
period of time, offering as an example the history of the chorus
in the Greek tragedy, from the "goat-song" of the incunabula
period of religious rites to the invention of the actor as someone
independent of the chorus, to the addition of several actors and
the relegation of the chorus to its now-familiar "backup" role.[8]
Yet Burke does not delve into the issue of how conventional
forms may be modified by the development of new and
different media. This is the principal contribution made by
Newcomb in his work on television, and it is in the spirit of

viewing this work as it may be absorbed into the Burkean view of form that I have offered a brief glimpse into Newcomb's ideas.

Shogun *on TV:*
Some Observations on Form

The rendering of *Shogun*, James Clavell's best-selling 1975 novel about seventeenth-century Japan, into a five-night television miniseries presents the popular culture critic with an appropriate sample of popular television fare to which we may apply many of the concepts discussed earlier in this chapter. Based upon the actual historical rise to power of the first warlord or "Shogun" to unify Japan, the television miniseries contains elements of both the traditional adventure, as it follows the exploits of the British navigator James Blackthorne (Richard Chamberlain), and the romance, as it chronicles the relationship between Blackthorne and Lady Mariko. The dynamics of the private affairs affecting the lives of the principal characters contrast with the events in the wider public arena, the struggle for power among various Japanese rulers and the involvement of the Portuguese Jesuits in the destiny-shaping events. Thus *Shogun* has many of the characteristics of the social melodrama, as defined by Cawelti.

Even to begin to summarize the plot of *Shogun* involves one in the observation that the plot structure was tailored to the television medium. As a miniseries running on consecutive evenings, *Shogun* presented its producers with the problem of maintaining an audience throughout the week. The formal structures had to be developed so that any evening's episode would not give off a sense of "finality" which would encourage audiences to abandon watching future episodes. Dramatic suspense had to be provided at the end of every evening, much the same as episodes of the old movie serials had "cliffhanger" endings which beckoned the audience to return the following week. At the close of the first three-hour episode, for example, we see Blackthorne in prison, being summoned by the executioner just after being told by a Spanish priest that no one is released from prison in Japan; everyone is either incarcerated indefinitely or executed. Even though the audience knows perfectly well that the series cannot run five evenings if Blackthorne dies by the second episode, a sense of curiosity forces audience members to tune in the second night. The audience is left to ponder several options: escape, sudden release, rescue, or some other solution.

As an "adventure" story with strong romantic subplots and dominant picaresque elements, *Shogun* alternates between public and private themes. As a "strategy for a situation," the situation being the maintenance of audience interest over a five-night span, it is important that the first evening start off powerfully, in order to build audience interest, with much emphasis on the public arena and the spectacle of a European Protestant navigator being stranded in a strange and terrifying country. Some of the most brutal incidents, subject of considerable attention from popular commentators, occurred during the first evening. These included the beheading of a peasant by a Samurai, Omi, who was piqued because the peasant had refused to bow in his presence, and the humiliation of Blackthorne by the same Samurai, who made him lie down and then urinated on him. These incidents are examples of repetitive form, helping to reinforce the historical setting and to strengthen the image the public had been sold on of the entire series as an action-oriented, violent, historical drama.

The second evening was an initiation into the more private relationships. After quickly establishing that Blackthorne has been released by a curious Lord Toranaga, we again meet Lady Mariko, whom we had a brief glimpse of the first evening. Mariko is appointed by Toranaga to serve as Blackthorne's interpreter, and we find the beginning of the attraction between them. We also explore the relationship between Toranaga as the strong and ambitious leader and Ishido as the plump and evil master of Osaka Castle in intimate castle scenes and in the suspenseful drama of Toranga's secret escape from the castle. The qualitative contrast between

Toranaga's overt use of his authority and Ishido's secretive and mysterious manipulation of people and events reinforces audience identification with Toranaga and suspicion of Ishido. Finally, we are also presented with the private plotting of the Jesuits and with the Portuguese seaman Rodrigues, a confused man torn between loyalty to faith and country and friendship for Blackthorne, whose personal qualities of intelligence and courage Rodrigues admires. In many ways, the second evening is the most diffuse of the episodes, yoking together so many disparate scenes of character development that the dramatic incidents (the attempted murder of Blackthorne in the castle, Toranga's escape, the sea battle at the mouth of the harbor, etc.) are almost overshadowed. The audience is left pondering what will follow, specifically what events will occur to yoke together the destinies of the various characters, whose thoughts and personalities are now more familiar. For the second evening, we find an "openness" to the structure, an openness which compels the audience to tune in the following evening.

The third episode is devoted principally to the romantic attraction between Blackthorne and Mariko, a major theme of which is the cultural indoctrination of Blackthorne (and the audience), in particular his exposure to the concept of *karma* or fate and the concomitant attitude that life exists in eternally present moments, not in the anticipation of future events. Blackthorne's "rebirth" in Japanese culture is accomplished when he very nearly commits *seppuku* or ritual suicide in an attempt to convince Lord Yabu to renounce his threat to destroy an entire village if Blackthorne doesn't become sufficiently proficient in Japanese. Only the intervention of Omi, Yabu's Samurai, saves Blackthorne's life.

The behavior of the Japanese characters is thus becoming more understandable to the American audience, since it is gradually being placed within a philosophical context, a context which hinges upon the formal development of the principal characters. The techniques of surprise and suspense, necessary to keep us interested in the action at an earlier stage, can now be replaced by more subtle techniques, such as dramatic irony. An audience unfamiliar with the cultural norms cannot be expected to adequately interpret information that may serve as a guide to future events, events that will occur as the plot unfolds. But an audience that is slowly informed about the Japanese belief systems and values can understand syllogistic progressions that hinge on Japanese notions. Such an audience can also be moved by qualitative progressions based on feelings motivated by non-Western values. We can now see that the most profitable view of *Shogun* through the third episode is one which views it as a working out of both qualitative and syllogistic progressions, each of which is necessary in a carefully planned "mix" if *Shogun* is to work for its audience. *Shogun* depends upon audience expectations of violence and action to *initially* draw viewers, even though the *real* project is considerably different. By the end of the third evening, the audience begins to miss the promised action. The formal structures, however, help propel the audience along as the indoctrination to Japanese values proceeds at a more rapid pace. Despite themselves, Western audiences begin to "think Japanese." One way by which *Shogun* helped audience identification with Blackthorne as protagonist was by presenting many conversations in Japanese, making the audience relate directly to Blackthorne's confusion and anxiety as he remained dependent on translation.

Thus by the third night, and with the aid of an episode focusing almost entirely on the explication of the Japanese value system, the audience is far enough advanced in its indoctrination that it can begin to "think in both cultures." The symbolic conclusion to this initiation process is the earthquake scene, where Blackthorne again saves Toranga's life, and the ceremony where he is made a Samurai. The qualitative progression which contrasts quiet scenes featuring Mariko's and Blackthorne's romantic attraction with the violent upheaval of the earthquake makes the episode stand out. Torangaga is appropriately "converted" to trusting in Blackthorne's good will precisely at the moment where Blackthorne—and the audience—stand ready to accept a Japanese world view. Fittingly, the episode ends quietly with

Mariko stressing the important values Blackthorne must now uphold as a Samurai.

The fourth evening's events serve to build up the tension needed for the denouement. Public and private events are brought together, and virtually every major character is highlighted to some extent, in symmetrical balance with their presence in the second episode. The principal public event is the summoning of Lord Toranaga to Osaka Castle by Lord Ishido and the Regents. The order is delivered by Toranaga's half brother, and the tension is enhanced by their blood relationship. Toranaga's acceptance of the order sets up audience expectations of a final confrontation between Toranaga and Ishido.

The private relationship between Blackthorne and Mariko is heightened by this anticipation of a public confrontation between Toranaga and Ishido and the possibility of death. The same sort of anxiety that accompanies the Toranaga/Ishido relationship becomes a psychologically important tool in qualitatively furthering audience anxiety in a scene where Mariko contemplates suicide after her husband, Buntaro, fails in an attempt at reconciliation with her. Mariko's near-death parallels Blackthorne's near-suicide of the previous evening, providing a "double" instance of qualitatively progressive form. The fact that both Mariko and Blackthorne have attempted suicide makes us feel that both are now leading "specially-charmed" fates wherein time is suspended. The capstone is the sexual culmination of their relationship as they journey to Osaka Castle and vow to remain lovers until they reach "the first bridge of Yedo."

This penultimate episode concludes with Blackthorne's request to Toranaga that Mariko be granted a divorce and be given permission to marry him. Toranaga's rage at Blackthorne's presumptuousness makes us ill at ease. The audience approaches the final evening with both public and private questions looming large: Will Toranaga be successful on the battlefield? Will Blackthrone and Mariko ever be allowed to find happiness with each other?

The final episode presents a series of events that

completely contradict the expectations of an audience accustomed to the patterned conclusion which would ordinarily be found in an adventure/romance story. Lord Yabu proves to be a traitor to Toranaga, setting up a night raid at Osaka Castle that results in Mariko's death. Blackthorne is temporarily blinded, is treated and aided by a group of Christian Samurai, and is ultimately rescued from Catholic Inquisitors by Rodrigues, whose admiration for Blackthorne's abilities finally outweighs his loyalty to Church. The expected battle scene between Toranaga and Ishido does not occur; instead the narrator tells us in a brief concluding voice-over that Toranaga ultimately won victory in battle and became Shogun.

The focus at the end is on Blackthorne as one who must accept a certain *karma*, a fate that decrees his remaining in Japan for the rest of his life. His ship has been burned on orders from Mariko (Blackthorne only belatedly learns this), and like a seventeenth century Tantalus, he is given money to rebuild his ship, never knowing that provisions have been made for the destruction of every new ship he may ever construct. The reinforcement of the concept of *karma* leaves the audience with an entirely different outlook on *Shogun*; by its conclusion, one walks away with the knowledge that the story is not "all about" adventuring and romance but rather about how conflicting social value systems have an impact on private lives.

Shogun is revealed to be a very unusual sort of social melodrama. The stress is upon how the protagonist comes to an understanding of how Oriental values work, as he experiences them against a backdrop of dramatic public action and private feeling. Instead of following Cawelti's formula of treating the "hidden motives, secret corruption, and human folly" underlying a familiar, contemporary, Western social institution, Clavell has chosen a time and place unfamiliar to most Westerners. Thus if we are to emerge from the total experience convinced that "God is in his heaven and all's right with the world," as Cawelti suggests is the proper attitude shaped by the social melodrama, we must undergo a double indoctrination, being exposed at once to the *surface values* espoused by the culture as well as to the inner contradictions.

The technique used to accomplish this audience indoctrination is to highlight the cultural differences by selecting a sympathetic protagonist with whom the audience can identify, and suddenly thrusting him into an alien culture. In *Shogun* Blackthorne is the sympathetic protagonist. We share his Western values and biases for the most part, and when he differs from us (as in his fervent anti-Papism), we understand the differences because they bear the marks of our own Western past. The presentation of much of the dialogue in Japanese is a stroke of genius, for it allows us to further identify with Blackthorne's bewilderment as he is confronted by a strange culture.

As Blackthorne develops in his understanding of the Japanese, so too do we develop. Repetitive form makes bits and pieces of the Japanese language sound familiar to our ears, so familiar that they are repeated by millions of *Shogun*-watchers in bars and factories all over America. Minor forms help reinforce our sense of Blackthorne's progress in becoming more Japanese. As an example of minor form, we may note the use of *contrast* in displaying Blackthorne's initial disdain for bathing as a custom "breeding disease" and contrasting this disdain with the scene involving the reunion with his men featured in the last episode. At the reunion, Blackthorne can scarcely contain his disgust at his crew's filthy habits and their stench, and he immediately bathes after leaving their midst.

The presence of the Portuguese Jesuits is an important element in the qualitative progression of the plot. Their value contradictions help prepare Western audiences for the seeming contradictions in Japanese culture since our own cultural background makes us more closely identify with the Jesuits, and makes us more disturbed when they behave in strange ways. An audience that observes Jesuit priests plotting the assassination of Blackthorne by Rodrigues in one scene and upholding a sacred vow not to reveal Blackthorne's request for Mariko's hand in marriage in another can better understand the mingled elements of courtliness and violence in Japanese society. Even for a modern Roman Catholic, the portrayal of the Jesuits symbolizes a culture just as alien to us and as complex as the Japanese.

Mariko's death represents the final moment in the cultural conditioning of the audience. If *Shogun* is to be perceived as an explication and "celebration" of a different culture instead of as a failed romance, the audience must be carefully prepared to accept the appropriateness of her fate. This preparation must be accomplished by the use of appropriate formal techniques. Mariko's death must be hinted at, it must be seen as a noble and "necessary" end, and provision must be made for Blackthorne to live on in a "happy" manner even after the passing. All of these ingredients are provided for within the formal structures of *Shogun*.

The near-suicides of both Blackthorne and Mariko, as we have already noted, allow both of them to lead a sort of "charmed" existence together. Life takes on a crystalline immediacy, a special presence, when one knows that one has been so close to death. Every moment becomes a special extension of life, rather than simply continuity of life, and so death, when it does occur, has less impact. An additional preparation for Mariko's end comes in her vow that the relationship with Blackthorne will end when they reach the first bridge of Yedo. Members of the audience may desire something else, but the vow foreshadows the possibility that something *will* interfere with the lovers finding ultimate fulfillment with one another.

Mariko's actual death represents a perfect syllogistic progression, a classic unraveling of fate, though it depends upon one factor—acceptance of the rules of the Japanese social system. Let us review the events leading up to her death; 1) It is a given fact that Ishido must give his permission for Mariko to leave Osaka Castle. 2) In order to fulfill her leige lord's (Toranaga's) orders, she *must* leave Osaka. 3) Ishido denies her permission to leave. 4) Mariko, caught between the horns of a dilemma, prepares herself for ritual suicide, the only socially acceptable way to resolve such a situation. 5) Ishido, who would be public y shamed by this, grants permission at the last minute, but 6) Mariko is too weakened by the lack of sleep and the emotional strain of being near death to leave that evening, so 7) Ishido forces Yabu ("Choose death or treason!") to help execute a night raid on Mariko's party 8) The night raid is successful, and Mariko is killed.

At each major point of decision for Mariko, the highest principles of loyalty, as they are expressed in feudal Japanese culture, are called into play. Her upholding of these values is noble, and her death is honorable. Ishido, on the other hand, is motivated by personal pride and a desire for power. Yabu, the traitor, chooses mere self-preservation, an ignoble motive. The chain of events is perfectly structured, and the values are compatible with Western ideals. The syllogism hinges, however, on the audience accepting that it is a genuine dilemma for Mariko to be forced between choosing loyalty to Toranaga and upholding the absolute custom of obtaining Ishido's permission before leaving his castle. Fortunately, four nights of cultural indoctrination brought about by the careful use of qualitatively progressive form have left the audience well prepared to accept this as a genuine existential dilemma. In general terms, Burke's model would show *Shogun* to be a drama where the minor forms of contrast and repetition build up a qualitative progression that serves to "graft" Japanese cultural values upon a Western audience, in order to "set up" the syllogistic progression that "explains" Mariko's death and gives it an almost tragic dimension.

Finally, we have the appropriately "tragic" restoration of order following Mariko's death. In the public arena, we hear of Toranaga's victory. In the private arena, we are assured that Blackthorne will find a measure of happiness with his assigned consort, Fujiko. A pivotal scene involves Fujiko calling his name and his momentarily turning his gaze, imagining her to be Mariko. The suggestion made here is that Fujiko, who has been loyal and accepting all along, will be a suitable mate. The fact that she has been chosen for him in the Japanese fashion further reinforces Blackthorne's total submersion into Japanese culture. On a symbolic level, Blackthorne and Fujiko are further united by the fact that both have been scarred by burns, she in the earthquake and he in the explosion that killed Mariko.

In sum, we may view *Shogun* as an elaborate contemporary social melodrama with a somewhat tragic dimension. This dimension hinges upon the indoctrination of the audience with the Oriental concept of *karma* or fate and the presentation of strong characters who achieve nobility in their acceptance of their *karma*. These factors are aided by a skillful blend of qualitative and syllogistic progressions. Qualitatively progressive form is appropriate since the social melodrama traditionally has an episodic plot which intermingles public and private events. In *Shogun,* this episodic structure is crafted to take advantage of the presentation via the medium of television and the scheduling of the broadcast over five consecutive evenings. The experience of American viewers with the vastly successful *Roots,* in particular, probably gave the producers of *Shogun* some idea of how to achieve a certain qualitative "effect" each evening, sometimes stressing the public arena of Samurai warfare and political intrigue and sometimes stressing the development of the private romantic relationship between Blackthorne and Mariko, just as *Roots* alternated between public events and private lives.

Dramatism provides us with considerable insight into *Shogun* because it bases its analysis of form on the premise that formal structures work in art because they communicate an author's intentions effectively by appealing to audience appetencies. A conventional analysis of *Shogun* may view it as too diffuse, so filled with minor characters and subplots that it fails by not showing us Toranaga's victory and by killing off the attractive heroine. A Dramatistic analysis reveals tremendous unity in the formal patterns of Shogun. The principal story line is allegorical; Shogun is really the story of a Westerner who gains true understanding of the seventeenth-century Japanese only by confronting the loss of his lover. Mariko's death is Christ-like in the sense that it serves as Blackthorne's redemption, making him "fit" to accept his *karma*. Because the popular television audience expects an action-adventure yarn, the formal structures must be carefully crafted so that the philosophical development of Oriental values does not proceed apace from the progressive transformation of the audience's expectations. Audience interest in the private relationships must rise as the public conflict fades. As we have seen, the use of minor forms such as repetition and contrast serve to aggregately build up qualitatively progressive structures allowing for value exploration. The logical calculus by which syllogistic progressive form hangs is thus "translated into Japanese," so that the audience can be ultimately prepared to understand Mariko's death.

Notes

[1] See for example John G. Cawelti, "The Concept of Formula in the Study of Popular Culture," *Journal of Popular Culture,* 3 (1969), pp. 381-90; "Notes Toward an Aesthetic of Popular Culture," *Journal of Popular Culture,* 5 (1971), pp. 255-68; *The Six-Gun Mystique* (Bowling Green, Ohio: Bowling Green University Popular Press, 1971); "Myth, Symbol, and Formula," *Journal of Popular Culture,* 8 (1974), pp. 1-9; *Adventure, Mystery, and Romance: Formula Stories as Art and Popular Culture* (Chicago: Univ. of Chicago Press, 1976). Hereinafter referred to as *Adventure;* subsequent reference citations will appear in parentheses in the text.

[2] Cawelti, "Myth, Symbol, and Formula," p. 4.

[3] Cawelti, "Myth, Symbol, and Formula," p. 4.

[4] Betty Cain has presented the idea of "multiple Pentads" applying to both artistic creation and audience response. See "Kenneth Burke's Four Pentads," in *Kenneth Burke in the Eighties: Where Are We Now?,* Southern California Occasional Papers in Rhetoric, No. I, ed. W. Ross Winterowd (Los Angeles: Univ. of Southern California Dept. of English, forthcoming).

[5] Horace Newcomb, *TV: The Most Popular Art* (Garden City, New York: Anchor Press/Doubleday, 1974), p. 23.

[6] Newcomb, p. 82.

[7] Newcomb, p. 256.

[8] Burke, pp. 205ff.

III

The Audience and Popular Art

Having examined the role of the artist and the nature of form in popular culture, we are at last ready to take up the final link in the communicative chain—the audience. As we noted in Chapter I, the motives underlying one's interest in a given work of art may vary tremendously. One individual may identify personally with the pattern of experience outlined by the work. Another may be a "fan" of a particular formula—the hard-boiled detective story, for example. A third may be seduced by a pattern of experience so foreign to his own that it proves intriguing. Despite these differences, one thing is clear: many works of popular art are able to attract and hold large, heterogeneous audiences.

The Dramatistic model proves an excellent heuristic for teasing out and organizing different patterns of audience response. If we examine the Act of experiencing and responding to a work of art, with the individual member of the audience serving as Agent, we find a series of distinctions emerging from a consideration of Purpose. In very general terms, if the Purpose underlying my experience of a work of art is to seek validation of my values and beliefs, I will be more enthralled by a work that features a protagonist whose pattern of experience is close to mine than I will by a work that promotes values alien to me. For example, the self-pitying poet's "The King and the Peasant" story (alluded to in Chapter II) would no doubt cause a starving artist to feel a strong sense of identification with the protagonist. In another case, my Purpose may be to seek information about some of the values and beliefs present in my culture. In this instance, I will be inclined to value works featuring unfamiliar patterns of experience, since there will be a "compensatory gain" in my becoming more familiar with other personalities, values, and customs.

A Dramatistic view of audience response to popular culture is thereby far removed from Abraham Kaplan's aesthetic approach discussed in Chapter I. Kaplan differentiated between a *reaction* and a *response*. A reaction is presented as a virtually behavioristic, predetermined result of being exposed to an external stimulus. Kaplan's model suggests that popular culture sets a course "laid out beforehand" for its audience to follow. The response to high art, on the other hand, supposes an audience possessed of free will, creatively melding the themes present in the work of art with their own values and patterns of experience.

Burke would view this model as dehumanizing. The *reaction* mode of Kaplan would find its place, in Burkean terms, in the world of *motion,* not *action.* The world of human thought and language, however, necessarily implies action, since it is a dialectical process of giving wings to motive, transcending the linear stimulus-response realm of mere motion (See *Grammar,* pp. 194-95). While granting that motion occurs in the purely biological activities of the body as they can be said to follow empirically-testable natural "laws," Burke argues firmly that any activity involving language, indeed, any *social* activity among humans, falls necessarily within the realm of action, since such behavior involves symbolic transformation. Thus even if a member of the audience were merely to recognize familiar values in a work of popular art, that act of strong identification with the material is one that can be just as fully explored with the tools of Dramatism as a different kind of response in which someone's entire value system is upset following an encounter with a work of art.

Countering Kaplan's implied suggestion that popular art merely reinforces the familiar is another notion widely held by critics of popular art, the belief that much popular art engages in unrealistic stereotyping which leads its audience away from the real world by distorting the lifestyles and values of certain classes of people. Critics of popular art who feature this belief in their writings are generally those who rant against the "escapist" elements of popular art, who argue that popular formulae will not prepare their audiences for experiences in the real world.

Burke easily counters both types of assumptions about popular art, noting that all art deals with life, not necessarily as it is led, but as it may be understood through the use of human symbols. As Burke notes:

> A fiction designed for an audience of workingmen...may give such pictures of life among the wealthy as could never be said by the wealthy to deal with life. But these pictures, however inaccurate, "deal with life" so long as they serve as Symbols for arousing in the workingmen such emotions *as the artist wished to arouse. (Statement,* p. 191.) (emphasis mine)

We see once again the stress upon the act of communication between artist and audience that I have pointed to all along. The artist selects a Symbol and ramifies it because he or she wishes to impart an idea to an audience. The work consists of formal structures reflecting conventions that have been established to help accomplish this aim. The audience approaches the work with some initial Purpose in mind (to learn something new, to have old values reinforced, to be amused, etc.) and either has this initial Purpose fulfilled or finds in the course of experiencing the work that he or she is led to share in a different sort of vision held by the artist.

Drawing upon Burke, we can outline a "Hierarchy of Response" that expands the term Identification. At the base would be a "pure" response to form, a parallel match-up between the sorts of repetitive activities of the body (such as the regularity of one's heartbeat) and the repetitive patterns in art. This type of response is universal and not dependent upon the development of unique patterns of experience for different people. It does involve identification in the sense that we become aware of the match-up between what is occurring to us physiologically and what is going on in the work of art. Repetitive body movements (head-wagging, fist-shaking, etc.) in response to the drum beat of primitive tribal music is a good example of this type of response. It is no small accident that nonlinguistic forms of art such as music engender this type of response much more powerfully than forms based in language. A cognitive bridge or internalized metaphor of some sort must be built in order to link the repetitive forms in poetry with more fundamental physiological processes such as heartbeat and respiration. It is fascinating, however, to note that in oral recitals it becomes evident how powerful repetitive form can be, even when expressed through the more "opaque" medium of human language.

The next level of response is that of personal identification with the patterns of experience symbolized in a work of art. One may identify strongly with a pattern expressed in the plot (the untimely death of an older brother) or in the development of a character (a Horatio Alger rags-to-riches story). Clearly there are all sorts of experiences which commonly occur to a great number of people, and on many occasions people who have undergone such experiences will identify strongly with them as they encounter them in works of art. The process of declaring a "match" between one's own experience and an experience presented in fictional form is a complex process of pattern recognition, much more elaborate than the "reaction" mode of Kaplan would suggest.

Conventional response would be one rung higher in the hierarchy, since it involves the member of the audience in a recognition of his participation in the social world. It is a common convention in many Western movies that the hero is a loner who saves a town from lawlessness only to ride away empty-handed, giving up the beautiful woman to the more domesticated rancher. This "man without woman" theme involves a special set of rules applying to a particular type of story form. The rules do not have to be written as such; one thinks of the medieval quest stories where the quester, after long journeys and many trials, is ultimately rewarded with riches and a fair lady. Yet the member of the audience, as a member of a social community, comes to identify with the conventional pattern as he or she experiences its recurrence in a number of works. The process is dialectical, thus allowing for the modification of old conventions and the establishment of new ones.

Finally, we have what might be called a "dynamic" response, a response where the audience encounters patterns or characters alien to their own experience. The usual Purpose for exposing oneself to such "alien" art is curiosity, the desire to widen one's knowledge of the world. I can think of an example from my own experience, my viewing the movie *American Gigolo*. I have never met a gigolo, and I doubt that I will encounter one soon, but the presentation of such a character on the screen allowed me to "identify with the Other" in a manner far less threatening than a real-life experience. The dynamic response thus allows a member of the audience to experience alien values and lifestyles vicariously, without the need for arousing natural defense mechanisms that inhibit one's ability to understand and empathize when faced with such experiences in everyday life.

It is important to note that *no experience* which can be symbolically transmitted by human art is entirely foreign to *anyone's* experience. This is true even for works far removed from us in time. Burke argues that historical relativists have made too much of the audience's inability to fully understand art from other ages. Any reader, Burke writes, "surrounds each word and each act in a work of art with a *unique* set of his own previous experiences" *(Statement,* p. 78). It is the considerable "margin of overlap" between any two people of different experiences that enables humans to communicate, dialectically arriving at some commonality. Communication is always incomplete, whether the gaps be historical, cultural, or psychological. Thus, Burke writes, "Absolute communication between ages is impossible in the same way that absolute communication between contemporaries is impossible" *(Statement,* p. 79).

At this juncture, we should anticipate and avoid any appearance of the "tail wagging the dog" by keeping in mind that form is the invention of writers and readers, not the other way around. Form has no life of its own outside of the human capacity to create and identify varying structures and to take pleasure in them. Epistemological considerations and questions concerning the root causes of this phenomenon aside, we note that audience response is essentially a dialectical "game" between a member of the audience and the work and simply acknowledge this capacity for delight in form to be true on the basis of our experience. The process of identifying with the Symbol presented by a work of art is really the process of "identifying" (in the sense of "naming") the forms present in the work, and cognitively unraveling how these forms are used by the artist to "court" the audience.

For Burke, the first step in understanding how form and audience interact is a search for the "key terms" which define the work. Burke asserts that "a Dramatistic approach to language vows us first of all to considerations of pure verbal internality, as we seek to chart the transformations within the work itself" (*Language,* p. 369). Here Burke is simply observing that when dealing with language, the human mind should seek to discover how associations are formed among clusters of terms, and how it is that, aggregately, these clusters exclude other clusters. To offer a simple example: If I mention "sunshine," "blue skies" and "gentle winds," one quickly gets the impression that I am focusing on the weather. This cluster of terms makes it fairly obvious to one of average intelligence that I am *not* talking about poker or Watergate or Kenneth Burke.

Burke outlines three stages for charting terms in fiction. The first is a raw count of the number of times a particular term appears and a "comparison of all the contexts in which a given word appears" (*Language,* p. 369.) Secondly, there are "radiations of a term." This is the process of building up the clusters of terms by noting how particular terms constantly appear and reappear with each other, building up "equations" that map the terms and observing how they overlap. This process of clustering leads us from word to theme, though

Burke cautions us to be aware of motivational distinctions between terms that seem synonymous (for instance, the use of favorable and unfavorable connotations of similar terms to draw distinctions between good and evil characters). Finally, Burke suggests that "subtitles" could be given to various parts of a poem or work of fiction, moving in stages as the reader progresses through the work, marking off the topics or themes that cluster together as the work unfolds. Though the titles given by the reader may not agree with those which would be given by the author or other readers, they do reveal the pathways that may be followed in getting to the essence of a work. Burke writes that:

> Each title would sum up the overall trend or spirit informing or infusing the range of details that are included under this head. And as we progressed from parts of chapters, to chapters, to groups of chapters, and so finally to an ultimate title of titles, we would have in effect a set of terms ever-widening in scope, until we got to the all-inclusive title that was technically the "god-term" for the whole congeries of words in their one particular order. (*Language*, p. 370.)

This process as described by Burke suggests a mode of response that is largely metonymic, in the sense of moving from specific terms to broad themes implied by these terms through the formulation of associational clusters.[1] It is worth noting that modern business firms use the statistical tool of factor analysis to achieve similar ends; in ascertaining "product image" as perceived by consumers, various statements made about a product are correlated with each other and grouped into "image clusters" that can be used by marketing specialists to discover what attributes of the product (size, shape, smell, packaging, etc.) appeal to various segments of the consuming public. In contrast with the more "left hemispheric" or "propositional" logic associated with metaphor, these metonymic, image-clustering activities have been associated with the "spatially oriented" right hemisphere of the brain. In "Brain, Rhetoric, and Style," W. Ross

Winterowd asserts that "there is good reason to characterize metaphoric interpretation as L[eft] H[emispheric], and there is equally good reason to characterize the interpretation of images as R[right] H[emispheric]."[2]

Winterowd argues that both hemispheres are necessary for the efficient processing of language. The right hemispheric talent of imaging, for example, is the easiest and best tool for deriving answers to such propositional, "left hemispheric" problems as: "Jim is taller than Bill. Who is shorter?" More importantly, the right hemisphere seems to be ideally suited for the synecdochic or metonymic use of images to invoke *cognitive categories*. Cognitive categories are simply the psychologist's means of describing the tendency of the mind to categorize, to inductively construct "ideal types" such as "mammals," "steamships," "professions," and the like. This process of image clustering in order to arrive at holistic meaning is precisely what Burke is driving at with his "statistical method" of charting key terms. It is a right hemispheric mode of unraveling meaning.

The left hemisphere is equally important, according to Winterowd. As Winterowd describes it, the left hemisphere is "the propositional side of the brain: it works well with deductive structures, handling the ghostliness of symbolic logic and the bare-bonedness of the syllogism and the sorites with a proficiency of which the RH is incapable."[3] In art, the left hemispheric structures function best when they help organize concrete details "served up" by the right hemisphere. Thus one of the reasons why metaphor, essentially a left hemispheric, "propositional" device, is so effective, is that it "propositionalizes *imagistically*."[4] "The night is a black bat," "Life is but a walking shadow," and so on.

Bi-hemisphericity also helps explain a paradox noted by Northrop Frye in his well-known essay, "Myth, Fiction, and Displacement."[5] Frye notes that the first reading of a work involves the sequential assembling of bits and pieces of information as the work "unfolds," chapter by chapter. Finally we arrive at the end, and from there the experience we have just had is lost forever as we come to grasp the mythic reality of the work as a whole. This mythic sense of the whole will pervade any and all future readings; even though we may again proceed sequentially through the work, there will never again be a "first time" when the incidents that occur in later chapters are completely unknown to us. Winterowd describes the process in terms of the brain's laterality as follows:

> The images (RH) are perceived in their temporal sequence (LH). In retrospect, the sequentiality of the images disappears, and the work becomes a gestalt (RH). Any one of the images becomes a synecdoche (RH) for the whole. In discussing *Moby Dick*, for instance, any one of its synecdochic images, frequently the substance of one chapter, can become "the point of entry"—"The Candles," "The Try-Works," "The Doubloon." In this sense, the mythos of the fiction is analogous to the cognitive category.[6]

Thus it is readily understood how our experiences of fiction, upon reflection, seems to be more of a "dreamy voyage" than a rational enterprise that can be conveniently recollected or duplicated. Recent brain theory may turn out to be leading us to the root of language's seeming ability to transcend the analytical boundaries suggested by mere words and syntax and present itself to the imagination holistically, through art.

Aspects of Response to Popular Art

There are certain aspects of audience response which seem to apply principally to the experience of works of popular art. A broad-based critical theory applied to a variety of popular art forms must be able to treat the similarities and differences in audience response to material presented by different media. It must also be able to deal with the apparent fact that mimetic forms are much more prevalent in popular art than in art designed for a more select audience. Finally, it must provide answers to the frequently-asked question: Does popular art *reflect* the values already present in mass society or does it *engender* them? I propose to take up these topics in the present section.

In Chapter I, we discussed Marshall McLuhan's theories that the media of communication were the most important factors in influencing audiences, more important than content, characterization, or form. To McLuhan, the medium *is* the message, since the effects each medium has on the human psyche are more powerful than the effects of content. Following this pathway of reasoning, McLuhan's research emphasizes the differences among media in terms of how they each help extend human senses—sight, sound, etc.—and in terms of the extent to which individual media appeal to particular senses to the exclusion of others. For example, film is so powerful visually that it elicits concentrated attention from the audience as the story unfolds continuously on the big screen. Through the camera, human eyes can travel faster and farther in a movie theater than they possibly can in the same span of time in real life. Human "experience" is therefore drastically changed by the medium.

One of my major objections to McLuhan is that he neglects the role of the artist and thus seems to forget that all art is basically an act of communication between an artist and an audience. In addition, I object to the "neutralizing" of such aspects of content as plot and characterization by the overemphasis on the role of the medium vis-a-vis form. In light of Burke's distinction between the stimulus-response mode of Motion versus the dialectical realm of Action, one might further find fault with McLuhan's theories on the grounds that they "dehumanize" the audience by making them victims of their nonsymbolic physiological responses to sensory stimuli. We need to recognize that *all* experience is brought to us through our senses, and that it is specious to hold that we are therefore robots who function only in the world of Motion. Humans have the ability to put sensory data back through the "black box" of their cognitive powers and transform them into symbolic material.

Granted the above, it is still true that differences in the medium of presentation can and do bring about differences in audience response. A common example comes to mind. How often do we hear the comment: "That movie was powerful when I saw it in the theater, but it just isn't right for television's small screen. The outdoor scenery lost its splendor and the musical score just wasn't as awesome." Clearly the medium of presentation *does* make differences. Rather than lay down an exhaustive list, let us simply note some of the more striking differences among media in terms of audience response.

I. *TIME:* Both in terms of "real time" experience of a work of art and "fictional time" as it may be presented in the work, media vary widely. We are "stuck" watching a film from beginning to end, and if we slip away to buy popcorn, we feel guilty at having missed out on a portion of the movie which cannot be recaptured except by viewing the entire work again. Television series have some of the same constraints, but as Horace Newcomb has noted, they have "continuity" in terms of familiar characters who reappear from week to week. Even if we miss an episode, we remain "in touch" with the characters. Novels, obviously, are self-contained. We can reread passages, skip ahead, and even read the conclusion first if we wish.

Fictional time is similarly different. Film has invented the "flashback" technique and the use of frequent "cuts" to effect a "montage" where small bits and pieces of events move rapidly before our eyes to simulate the rapid passage of time. Television has similar techniques, but in written fiction, the words alone can be used quite handily to indicate the passage of time or even to reverse the flow of time. We may skip around in time as we follow characters in fiction, but this technique, first tried with a mass audience in the 1967 film, *Two for the Road,* is difficult to carry off in cinema. In this film, the audience is presented with a portrait of a disintegrating marriage, revealed by exposing a series of vignettes, highlighting vacation trips made by the couple (Audrey Hepburn and Albert Finney) over a span of several years. The vignettes flash back and forth in time, and the potential for audience confusion is great. Fortunately, the film provides clues to the chronology. As time passes, the obvious increase in the couple's income and social standing is symbolized by their wearing more sophisticated clothing and driving more expensive cars. The audience is also oriented by changes in hairstyle and makeup, and by the couple's ability to afford increasingly more expensive vacation spots.

II. *INTERIOR THOUGHT:* It is relatively easy to present interior monologue in a written work; the author simply states that so-and-so thought such-and-such, and provided that there is consistency in narrative mode (the third person, omniscient narrator is required for this), the audience readily follows along with little or no objection to being taken on a tour inside someone's brain. Writers such as William Faulkner have perfected the art of presenting interior thought, so that in a novel such as *The Sound and the Fury* we are allowed to accompany the imbecile Benjie as he "experiences" and remembers the outside world.

Film and television are completely different. It is difficult to present interior thought in these media without seeming a bit silly; one readily thinks of the organ music and whispered monologue representative of those moments in daytime TV soap opera when we are exposed to a character's innermost thoughts. The French have done better, at least with the rise of New Wave cinema in the late Fifties and Sixties. A common device in these films is the dream; fog, filters, lens distortion, shifts from black-and-white to color or vice versa, and other cinematographic techniques provide a surrealistic *mise-en-scene* as we follow a character's innermost feelings as revealed through his dreams. A similar technique was used in a more widely viewed work, Stanley Kubrick's film version of *A Clockwork Orange.* In order to enhance the suggestion that the principal character was violently insane, Kubrick used a wide-angle lens on various interior shots taken from the character's point-of-view. At close range, a wide-angle lens distorts subjects considerably. This visual distortion, present every time we witness something from the point-of-view of the insane protagonist, symbolically parallels his "distorted perspective" on the real world. Modern audiences, by exposure to these sorts of films, are now trained to look for various types of cinematographic tricks as evidence that they are being exposed to "subjective" states of consciousness. In that sense, they are more "literate" in reading these "cinematic conventions" than previous generations of film-goers.

III. *PORTABILITY:* Books and magazines can be carried to a variety of places, and thus are often used by audiences in settings where it would be impossible to have films or television. Thousands of office workers pack away popular novels to read during their lunch breaks, and to the extent that their Purpose for experiencing these works is a function of the portable nature of the book, portability is a significant factor in audience response. Films are not only much less portable; they also are seen in the company of a large audience. The experience is different in the sense that the reactions of a member of the audience are less personal; the individual is influenced to some extent by the reactions of the group.

With television, on the other hand, the audience is considerably smaller (usually a family group), but the commercial breaks seem to have conditioned TV audiences to be able to readily switch their attention on and off at will. The redundancy built into most television plots seems to be a recognition of the fact that many members of the audience are not giving the program their full attention.[7]

To sum up, it is clear that differences among the major media used for popular art do exist and do influence the experience of popular art by mass audiences. In the Dramatistic model, the medium of presentation would be a "sub-Agency" used by the artist as Agent. The primary Agency would be human language and conventional form, the latter differing somewhat depending on differences in medium. The same symbol can be presented in a variety of media, with the same ramifications and the same patterns of experience. To this extent, Dramatism stands opposed to McLuhan's theories, suggesting that differences in medium of presentation are perhaps matters best dealt with under the classical rhetorical department of Delivery.

Turning from considerations of media to reflections upon content, we take note of the fact that a great deal of popular art—science fiction being a sometimes noteworthy exception—is mimetic. Recognizable people perform recognizable tasks in recognizable surroundings. Dialogue is generally fashioned from plain speech. Ordinary events do not suddenly become surreal, as they do, say, in the short stories of Donald Barthelme. Characters are motivated by love, envy, greed, ambition, thirst for justice. Even when the extraordinary is presented, as in Richard Dreyfuss' compulsion to journey to the aliens' landing spot in *Close Encounters of the Third Kind,* the characters are surrounded by various emblems and ornaments of everyday life. Dreyfuss, in *Close Encounters,* has an ordinary job as an electrical lineman, an ordinary family with a wife and two kids, and an ordinary house in a suburban neighborhood.

Critics of popular art have frequently used the fact that mimesis is the predominant mode in popular art as a sign of its simplicity. Abraham Kaplan and others have used the presence of the ordinary aspects of life in popular art to bolster their arguments that popular culure merely *reflects* values already present in society, and hence offers a passive experience to the audience. Kaplan forgets a crucial aesthetic distinction that Burke reminds us of in *Counter-Statement* (See *Statement,* pp. 7-9.) Value can exist in both an "art-to-display-art" aesthetic and an "art-to-conceal-art" aesthetic. Elements of form are highlighted in art-to-display-art, while realistic details drawn from real life are stressed in art-to-conceal-art.

From a Dramatistic perspective, we find that critics such as Kaplan have lost sight of the Purpose with which the popular artist uses mimetic elements. Aspects of the ordinary world are most often presented in popular art because they facilitate *audience identification* with the patterns of experience symbolized by the work. The familiar world is presented from the distance made possible by art, and audiences are thereby invited to participate in an exploration of the values present in their society. At the end of the voyage they may be persuaded to agree to the values or to find fault with them, but the fact that the experience itself involves active participation with the work and cognitive transmutation of pieces of language or bits of flickering light should not be overlooked or undervalued.

One contemporary critic argues that popular art has been undervalued because it represents a Classical style in an age just emerging from the prescriptive norms of Romanticism. British film critic Raymond Durgnat writes that the popular artist is not attempting to express his personal feelings when he creates a work of popular art. Nor is he following the Expressionist "art for art's sake" dictum that the experience of creation is what counts, not the final product. Rather, the popular artist

> aims neither to communicate his own individual feelings to others, nor to give himself a workout in artistic activity, but to express other people's feelings for them. It's true that he can only know their feelings via his own. It's true that he's not an objective machine and that his feelings are bound to influence his picture of theirs. None the less he uses his own feelings as a way of tracking other people's. His self-expression is accidental, one almost feels as if he would like to be invisible.[8]

Durgnat's concept is close to what Kenneth Burke means by the term "courtship." Burke defines courtship as "the use of suasive devices for the transcending of social estrangement."[9] The key words here are "suasive devices." To Burke, these devices include all the aspects of form outlined in *Counter-Statement:* repetitive form, syllogistic and qualitatively progressive form, and the various minor forms. Popular artists use the details of everyday life to grab the attention of mass audiences and focus it on the symbol; they are "strategies for situations" whereby an appetite is created and fulfilled. Artists who create for elite audiences can afford to be more idiosyncratic because their audiences have been trained to respond to the unusual. The ordinary folk who make up mass audiences are not specialists. They have in common only the world of mass culture and the occurrences common to all human lives—birth, death, family relationships, etc. The popular artist recognizes this and uses these aspects of the ordinary world as a set of "suasive devices" to court the audience.

The Burkean model thus provides a tentative answer to the frequently posed question as to whether popular art reflects or engenders social values and mores. Dramatism would suggest that it does both. Popular art reflects social values because it presents universal patterns of experience, patterns that the artist must recognize in order to fashion the work and that the audience must recognize if it is to "understand" the work. It engenders values by presenting dramatic scenarios placing ordinary values in conflict situations, situations demanding that some hierarchy of values be established, and by stimulating audience identification with the processes of value formation. Mimetic elements can thus be seen as a function of the overall Act of communication and courtship between artist and audience, not as the end-all, be-all of popular art.

The Dead Zone: *Supernatural Novel for an Empirically Minded Audience*

Stephen King's 1979 novel, *The Dead Zone,* is an attempt to portray a psychic with powers of precognition to an audience presumed to be highly skeptical. King is best known as the author of *Carrie* and *The Shining,* both of which were made into major motion pictures. As a specialist in popular novels dealing with parapsychological phenomena, alien states of being, and plain, old-fashioned horror, King is adept at creating realistic characters and settings designed to make the macabre more credible in the eyes of those who grew up believing in the scientific method.

The Dead Zone centers on the thoughts and deeds of Johnny Smith, a young New England schoolteacher who spends four and one-half years in a coma following an auto accident and who awakens to discover that he has extraordinary psychic abilities. While still in his hospital bed, he informs his physician, Dr. Weizak, that the latter's mother had not died at the hands of the Nazis in World War II, as Weizak had always believed, but that she had escaped, married again, and eventually settled in California. Later, Johnny assists a small town sheriff in locating a brutal, psychotic murderer. Shunning the resultant publicity, he takes a job as a private tutor for Chuck Chatsworth, son of a wealthy industrialist, only to see his psychic abilities break to the surface once again when he saves Chuck's life by predicting that a roadside inn scheduled to host Chuck's graduation party will burn to the ground during the celebration. Finally, after fleeing to the West for several months in the wake of even more publicity, Johnny returns to New England, obsessed with the memory of meeting a corrupt Congressman from New Hampshire. This meeting had convinced Johnny that the Congressman would one day become President of the United States and lead the nation toward a nuclear holocaust. Ultimately, Johnny decides that this knowledge is too much to bear, and convinced that no one will believe his psychic prediction of the holocaust, he takes it upon himself to assassinate the Congressman.

The Dead Zone is fast-paced, and as the brief plot summary above attests, it contains a panoply of events. Indeed, the most interesting aspect of the novel is that is is clearly written for a broad, general audience, not just one that already comes with a propensity for enjoying tales of the supernatural. The details all contribute to the character development and help establish a realistic backdrop for the more unusual events. In Dramatistic terms, the challenge that King faces is one of building audience identification with a protagonist who has supernatural powers. The formal structures that help build such identification must also help overcome the skepticism of those audience members who resist a "willing suspension of disbelief" in the supernatural.

In building Johnny Smith's character, King especially focuses on the effects that the lengthy coma has had on Johnny's relationship with his girlfriend—who has married someone else during his long period of illness—and on his relationship with his parents. His sad acceptance that Sarah Hazlett could not wait forever for him to awaken when all odds were against his recovery helps reveal Johnny as a sensitive, loving individual. Similarly, Johnny is kind towards his mother, even though she has psychologically "cracked," defending herself against thoughts of losing her only son by immersing herself deeper and deeper in religious extremism, going so far as to join "The American Society of the Last Times," a small group of fanatics who have plans to buy a farm and there await the arrival of extraterrestrial beings who supposedly had communicated with them telepathically.

These pseudoreligious beliefs are an important element in understanding how King is able to convince his audience that Johnny's psychic abilities are perfectly plausible. By placing Johnny's relatively "tame" powers in a middle ground between Vera Smith's extraterrestrial evangelism and the scientific skepticism of medical doctors and reporters, King makes them more accessible to a large audience. Vera Smith serves as a foil, becoming the scapegoat for those who would enjoy denouncing the purely fantastic. Rigid scientific empiricism, on the other hand, also comes under suspicion for failing to allow for the possibility of a metaphysical world. The empirical point of view is enunciated by Dr. Jim Brown, one of the two physicians treating Johnny, following the incident where Johnny locates Dr. Weizak's long-lost mother. Weizak, who is a sympathetic believer in Johnny's powers, tells him that Brown cannot be judged too harshly for his failure to believe:

> He thinks you are having us on. Making things up for some reason of your own. Seeking attention, perhaps. Don't judge him solely on that, John. His cast of mind makes it impossible for him to think otherwise. If you feel anything for Jim, feel a little pity. He is a brilliant man, and he will go far.... But he is curiously limited. He is a mechanic of the brain. He has cut it to pieces with his scalpel and found no soul. Therefore there is none. Like the Russian astronauts who circled the earth and did not see God. It is the empiricism of the mechanic, and a mechanic is only a child with superior motor control.[10]

This argument lays the groundwork for the audience believing in the possibility that an accident similar to Johnny's could, in fact, cause someone to have parapsychological powers. The ethos projected by Dr. Weizak helps "sell" the audience on the premise, since he is presented as a sympathetic, "objective" analyst. As does *Shogun, The Dead Zone* uses minor characters as foils to promote audience identification with particular values.

Close identification with Johnny's fate is further aided by the clustering of details which expand the sense that Johnny has an unfortunate fate and that make his psychic abilities seem like a curse rather than a blessing. Ordinary readers can sympathize with Johnny's sorrow over missing his chance for love with Sarah, his admixture of guilt and pity over his mother's self-destructive religious beliefs and her neglect in taking her prescribed medicine, and the isolation caused by his "Midas touch" that turns most physical contact with other humans into psychic experiences. Johnny becomes an outcast from the society he loves, alone, miserable, haunted by reporters. Sharing the experience of these ordinary feelings helps the reader become seduced into accepting Johnny's *total* pattern of experience, supernatural phenomena and all. In Dramatistic terms, these experiences help "ramify the Symbol" of Johnny as an unfortunate victim.

The suspense builds as the novel moves toward the fated confrontation between Johnny and Congressman Stillson. King has previously established Stillson as a clearcut villain by splicing several chapters tracking various stages of Stillson's career into the primary narrative of Johnny's experience. This is an interesting use of the "cross-cutting" technique frequently used in film to display two or more separate events occurring in different locations at the same time. In *The Dead Zone* the effect is similar to the "cross-cut" shot of the villain in the melodrama, twisting his mustache as the heroine lies tied to the railroad tracks. Thus as we build up sympathy for Johnny, we are given glimpses of the evil Stillson. This technique virtually "goads" the audience into "sneering" at Stillson. Specifically, the audience is presented with snapshots of Stillson as a young, duplicitous Bible salesman in the Midwest, viciously kicking a farmer's dog to death, and as a sleazy small town businessman who uses supposedly reformed motorcycle gang members as "muscle" whenever mere persuasion fails to work. The fact that such a man could be elected to Congress as a populist, independent candidate is explained by the fact that he capitalizes on post-Watergate fears about experienced Washingtonians. This strikes a note of historical accuracy; the possibility of such an implausible character being elected bears comparison with the smooth rise of fascism in Sinclair Lewis' *It Can't Happen Here.*

The first meeting between Johnny and Stillson does not occur until the reader is three-fourths of the way through the novel. Until that point, the reader is aware that Stillson is fated to play an important role in the denouement, but the exact nature of that role has not been established. In Chapter 20, however, Johnny attends a campaign rally and in the bustle of the crowd briefly comes into physical contact with Stillson. Johnny's precognitive powers are usually stimulated by touch, and with Stillson the narrator tells us that:

> For Johnny it had never been this strong, never. Everything came to him at once, crammed together and screaming like some terrible black freight train highballing through a narrow tunnel, a speeding engine with a single glaring headlamp mounted up front, and the headlamp was *knowing everything,* and its light impaled Johnny Smith like a bug on a pin. There was nowhere to run and perfect knowledge ran him down, plastered him as flat as a sheet of paper while that night-running train raced over him.
>
> He felt like screaming, but had no taste for it, no voice for it.
>
> The one image he never escaped
> (*as the blue filter began to creep in*)
> was Greg Stillson taking the oath of office.[11]

The imagery, the shift in tone and variation in point of view—from objective, third-person narrator to the interior thoughts of Johnny—and the emphasis on Johnny's being a victim of his own "perfect knowledge," all enhance the intensity of the experience.

What follows is a series of incidents that cement Johnny's fate. Shortly after the meeting with Stillson comes Johnny's prediction of the graduation party fire. When his vision comes true, Johnny flees from the resulting publicity, taking on a new identity in Arizona. But he is haunted by his vision of Stillson becoming President and by the knowledge that no one had believed his previous predictions until *after* they had come true. Upset by the fact that most people fail to distinguish between the "valid" powers of precognition that he possesses and the demented ramblings of disordered fanatics such as his mother, he concludes that no act of public persuasion or internal disruption of Stillson's political organization will work. He sees assassination as the only viable alternative. His resolve is enhanced when he discovers that he has a fatal brain tumor associated with his accident and with his powers, and he journeys back to New England for the final confrontation, knowing that this deed must be accomplished before the sands of time run out.

The denouement is thus "set up" by a set of logical steps that depend upon the audience identifying with Johnny as a protagonist and "believing in" his parapsychological powers. In order to enjoy the novel, one must "cross the line" from being a skeptic to being a supporter, since the skeptics would help put a fascist in office.   The confrontation with Stillson occurs in an old New England town hall. Johnny creeps into an upper loft with a rifle, prepared to kill Stillson as the Congressman addresses a public meeting, but his plans go awry. Johnny turns out to be a poor marksman, and he winds up being shot by Stillson's guards. Ironically, though, Stillson had grabbed a small boy in a blue sweater (the "blue filter" of Johnny's precognitive vision) during the shooting and held him up before him as protection. This act of cowardice was captured by an amateur photographer and widely reprinted, ruining Stillson's career. Johnny's intentions were thus fulfilled, despite their not working out as planned.

What is most striking about Stephen King's writing in *The*

Dead Zone is his ability to create a set of logical conditions that aid audience identification with actions that violate social norms. We have already seen how King makes Johnny's supernatural powers seem plausible by contrasting them with the "purely kooky" behavior of Vera Smith and the stuffy scientism of Dr. Brown. But in order to agree to the appropriateness of Johnny's decision to assassinate Stillson, the reader must be convinced—at least within the fictional framework—that Johnny's powers are absolutely trustworthy and that he is a reliable judge of right and wrong. This is primarily accomplished by highlighting Johnny's sense of being the victim of his abilities and by demonstrating that he only chooses to use them altruistically. Johnny rejects a lucrative job offer as a psychic columnist for *Inside View* (a thinly guised substitute for the *National Enquirer)*, preferring to remain in the teaching profession. But the publicity following the Castle Rock Strangler case causes him to lose his teaching job. Alone and depressed, cut off from physical contact by those who fear what Johnny may discover about them by merely touching them, Johnny has the perfect pattern of experience for an assassin. But by making his powers credible and by making him a sympathetic "mysterious stranger" figure who is the victim of a strange fate, Stephen King convinces the audience that Johnny's final act is one of martyrdom.

The "conversion" of the audience to a set of values applauding an act of planned murder suggests that works of popular art can accomplish far more than simply reinforcing familiar beliefs. As a tale of the supernatural, *The Dead Zone* is representative of its formula type as John Cawelti describes it when he writes that for the story dealing with alien beings or states, "the underlying moral fantasy is our dream that the unknowable can be known and related to in some meaningful fashion" (*Adventure,*p. 49). But it goes beyond its type insofar as it also serves the purpose of challenging our presumptions concerning political assassination. In the post-Kennedy/King era, it would be safe to say that most people believe that assassination is an inappropriate way to deal with despotism.

Stephen King roughs up this belief by providing us with a moral fantasy in which we identify with the assassin as a hero who prevents the ultimate destruction of human values, nuclear war. To kill a morally debased person whose conniving or incompetence would lead inevitably to holocaust is presented as an acceptable value.

If we relate back to the "hierarchy of response" outlined earlier in this chapter, we find that *The Dead Zone* invites the "highest" level of response, the "dynamic" level. Cawelti's formula prescription for stories of alien beings or states would explain the audience's being able to relate to Johnny's psychic powers. This would be an instance of "conventional" response. However, for the audience to assent to the appropriateness of Johnny's assassination attempt, there must be a "deeper" involvement, a *dynamic* involvement with the value conflicts raised by the work. To this extent, *The Dead Zone* provides a serious challenge to Abraham Kaplan's distinction between "reactions" and "responses."

We are left, therefore, with the challenging thought that audience response to popular art is every bit as complex as the response to high art. If standard values and preconceived notions may be roughed up by popular art, then what is there that distinguishes audience response to high art? From a Dramatistic perspective, the difference may lie in the *Scene* within which the audience exists. The audience for high art, as Gans has noted, tends to be "creator-oriented," with a great deal of knowledge concerning an artist's background and his aims. The popular audience, on the other hand, tends to be oriented toward a set of conventional social values that serve as a background Scene for popular art. Thus, to refer back to Durgnat's distinction, the audience for high art may be better equipped—*by virtue of their training and exposure*—to relate to the "Romantic ethos" of high culture. In popular art, the "Classically minded" artist must rely on formal structures and appealing themes to "court" the mass audience.

Notes

[1] Burke writes: "Such a process of abbreviation, whereby some one element of a context can come to be felt as summing up a whole, is no rarity. It is a normal resource of the representative function that the old rhetoricians called synecdoche, the resource whereby a part can come to stand for a whole." (*Language*, p. 371)

[2] W. Ross Winterowd, "Brain, Rhetoric, and Style," in *Linguistics, Stylistics, and the Teaching of Composition*, ed. Donald McQuade (Akron, Ohio: Univ. of Akron, 1979), p. 167. An interesting study which supports this thesis and which suggests that image interpretation may play a part in our understanding of metaphors has been reported by psychologists Howard Gardner and Ellen Winner. (See Gardner and Winner, "The Development of Metaphoric Competence: Implications for Humanistic Disciplines," *Critical Inquiry*, 5 (1978), 123-41.) The researchers noted that patients with right hemisphere brain injuries were unable to correctly identify pictures designed to illustrate such common metaphors as "He wore a loud tie," or "He had a heavy heart." In sharp contrast to those with left hemisphere injuries and to a normal control group, the right hemisphere patients were attracted to literal images (e.g., a tie with noise emanating from it) rather than to images correctly corresponding to the meaning of the metaphor.

[3] Winterwod, p. 156.

[4] Winterowd, p. 166.

[5] Northrop Frye, "Myth, Fiction, and Displacement," in *Fables of Identity* (New York: Harcourt Brace Jovanovich, 1963).

[6] Winterowd, p. 172.

[7] As a side note, I offer the personal and perhaps subjective observation that film audiences in the last ten or fifteen years seem to be noisier and more restless; my guess is that some of the behavior patterns developed from watching television have crept into the movie theaters.

[8] Raymond Durgnat, "Art and Audience," *British Journal of Aesthetics*, 10 (1970), p. 18.

[9] Kenneth Burke, *A Rhetoric of Motives* (1950; rpt. Berkeley: Univ. of California Press, 1969), p. 208.

[10] Stephen King, *The Dead Zone* (New York: New American Library, 1979), p. 127.

[11] King, pp. 303-04.

IV
Alembication

Students of Burke will understand why I have substituted "Alembication" in place of the more traditional title given to a concluding chapter, "Summary and Conclusions," since it is a term frequently used by Burke to imagistically symbolize the distillation process whereby human reason tries to make sense of the human environment by means of language. It is simply impossible to "summarize" or "conclude" when dealing with Burke. Dramatism provides us with a seemingly endless array of stages from which to perform our analysis of human action. By enlarging or reducing the scope of our endeavors, as we have done throughout the present work, we can use the Dramatistic method to reveal almost any sort of relationship. A film script can be viewed as an opportunity to present a new hero model to future-shocked Americans. The death of a beautiful Oriental lady can become a more powerful symbol to transmit Japanese cultural values to American audiences than the dramatic rise to power of a feudal warlord. The scientific empiricism of the post-Sputnik generation can serve as a Scene of sedimented social values craftily invaded by a skilled teller of supernatural tales. Thus as we pause to assess the implications of this volume, we arrive at a moment where the ideas put forward are not so much "summarized" as they are "distilled" or "alembicated."

One concept that has distilled in the process of this work is a new appreciation for the complexities of popular art. Only twenty years ago most scholars approached the subject of popular art very cautiously. Popular art was characterized as being the degradation of taste, the cheapening of quality. The popular artist was seldom paid attention to, though whenever he or she *did* enter the picture, it was usually as a vulgar cartoon villain, a commercializer who placed the Almighty Dollar ahead of true concern for art. Popular art was said to have no form; it was merely spectacle, like a Las Vegas revue, attracting audiences by appealing to the "lowest common denominator" elements—sex, violence and cheap sentiment. Members of the audience were either lowbrow Neanderthals or pitiable victims of a subversive movement designed to cheapen cultural values and aesthetic taste.

Our new, Dramatistic outlook on popular art would view it as the "glue" that helps a society hold to a common center. By transmitting cultural values to a mass audience and by providing a nonthreatening forum whereby these values can be exposed, challenged and refined, popular art serves the "classical" function of making clearer a society's axiomatic assumptions and root beliefs. Popular art becomes a cooperative venture between the popular artist and society; the creator of popular art is praised for his or her efforts to communicate to a large, heterogeneous audience rather than condemned for making money at the task.

The traditional concept of "aesthetic distance" begins to evaporate under our new model, since popular art demands close involvement with the material as it is used as a utilitarian tool for living. Popular audiences do not seek to "block out" the external world when they encounter popular art. Rather, they must bring in every facet of the external world to aid in interpretation. The signs, totems, and taboos of ordinary existence help establish heroes and villains; if John Travolta wears "Frye" brand cowboy boots, then he must be "cool." Rather than condemning such behavior, the Dramatistic popular art critic recognizes that signs and totems have always served as social navigation aids, to primitive clans and modern suburbanites alike.

It is this recognition of the social nature of art that gives Dramatism a special advantage over other methodologies. The reader may perhaps have gotten the impression that some of the critics and theorists mentioned throughout this study are supposed to be "bad guys" or "good guys." McLuhan, one

might deduce, is a "bad guy" because he practically breathes
life into stone-cold media and in the process of so doing nearly
forgets the artist ever existed. Kaplan may be seen as another
"black hatted" critic for his arrogance in treating popular
audiences as if they were all passive receptacles for mass-
marketed trash. Cawelti, on the other hand, would be a
"Deputy Sheriff," whose work on popular formulae proves to be
rather compatible with the Dramatistic method.

If the reader *has* gotten the impression that these critics
should be classed as heroes or villains, then the reader is
wrong. My purpose throughout has been to show that
Dramatism is a superior methodology in treating popular art,
superior because it covers more ground than other methods,
not to cast out earlier critics from the sacred ground. Marshall
McLuhan, Herbert Gans and others have had a serious interest
in popular arts, having done much to lead the study of popular
art out of the critical wasteland of the masscult era. I have
compared them with Burke throughout this study merely to
show the relevance of Burke and to reveal the difference
between the broad territory he covers and the narrower ground
staked out by the critical luminaries of the recent past.
Ultimately, Dramatism unearths more similarities than
differences between popular art and "high" art. That others
have not quite succeeded in demonstrating this is
understandable, since not everyone, to be sure, can accept the
mission that Stanley Edgar Hyman sees as Burke's, "to do no
less than to integrate all man's knowledge into one workable
critical frame."[1]

In the present study, we have charted some of the principal
landmarks of this integrative frame. Although the
organization of the preceding three chapters has been
traditionally rhetorical in that it follows the three major
components of the department of invention—ethos, logos and
pathos—in each chapter we have seen the interdependency of
the three. The artist must have a vision of the audience, a
notion of what elements in the work of art will promote greater
identification with the work, before he or she even sets out to
create. Likewise, in experiencing the work, the audience is

forced to attend to the symbolic ramifications placed there by the artist. As Burke puts it:

> A book in itself is a symbolic act of synthesis. The writer of the book is in a personal situation involving a myriad different factors. His own particular combination is unique—and the book that has engrossed him is the summing-up of this unique combination. But though his situation is unique, it is in many ways *like* the situation of other people. Hence, their modes of summing-up will manifest patterns that correspond with his.[2]

Works of art are the *loci* where public and private modes of being meet. The sharing of symbols between art and audience is a "transcending upward," to use another of Burke's phrases, from the solipsism of the mind's inner workings to the communal knowledge, dialectically achieved, that other minds do, in fact, experience things as ours do.

Dramatism is, arguably, the best methodology for the study of popular art because it is descriptive, not evaluative. Burke's terminology—"analytic radiations," "perspective by incongruity," "ratios of the Pentad"—points to the open stance of Dramatism. Many critics start from a closed stance, a set of axioms which attempt to define precisely the relationships among artist, work and audience. To dig beneath the surface observations of various schools of criticism is to unearth various sets of philosophical assumptions. The New Critics, for example, consciously or unconsciously all adopt the premise that epistemology is at best limited to self-understanding. The artist's private associations and attitudes cannot be shared with the audience, and vice versa; therefore, speculation on such attitudes should not be included in critical discussion. The Dramatist, on the other hand, shares with Whitehead a concern for the "problem of other minds." Propinquity, the Dramatist suggests, physically, temporally, spiritually, culturally, psychologically, and otherwise, makes the inner life of individual experience a lot more "knowable" than epistemological skeptics would suggest. Dramatism assumes, at its base, that *all* human understanding is tentative, whether it is understanding of the self, of the world, or of other human beings. "Understanding" is not fixed at some point in one's life or in the life of a society, but rather is constantly evolving, dialectically, through the searching playfulness of humans using their powers of symbolic transformation to make sense of a raw, unfiltered, unpatterned universe.

Thus Burke's root axiom is that all knowing is provisional. There will always be the possibility of a more complete understanding of everything, since no human mind can ever possibly have a complete grasp of all the ramifications of even a single event or object. Self-understanding, for Burke, can never really be said to be any more complete than one's understanding of others. Thus rather than artifically divide the process of artistic creation and the process of audience response, why not try to come up with an expansive, open-framed methodology that can "tease out" the common elements of both processes and show their interrelationship. Dramatism is the result.

In the first chapter of this study, I briefly discussed some of the principal critical methods used during the past twenty years to study popular art. In that chapter I argued that Dramatism was a more comprehensive methodology for the study of popular art than earlier approaches, and I used the tools of the Pentad to poke and prod at some of the *lacunae* of these earlier methods. At this point, however, I find myself more concerned with the future of the study of popular arts than with its past. In the bluntest of terms, I find that popular arts study has reached a point of alarming stagnation.

In the late Sixties and early Seventies, young scholars began to break free from an unwritten rule that said nothing scholarly should be done until a work of art or a historical event had become firmly cemented by the passage of time. In literary scholarship, this rule was the familiar dictum laid down by Matthew Arnold that a work could not be judged as great until at least a century had passed. The Arnoldian dictum began to fade in the Twenties and Thirties with the admission of American and early modernist literature to the canon, but it took the general spirit of rebellion in the Sixties, which took hold of scholars almost as firmly as it took hold of political activists, to bring about the first college-level courses in popular culture. The students' cry for a "relevant" curriculum was answered, in part, by the devising of courses in science fiction and the aesthetics of Alfred Hitchcock films.

Unfortunately, the band of scholars who are seriously interested in popular art has remained rather small, and they are, for the most part, an inbred group of dedicated popular culture aficionados who turn their after-hours hobbyhorses— detective novels, radio evangelism, images of women in daytime TV serials and the like—into topics for papers at Popular Culture Association meetings. Hidden away in obscure corners in various departments—English, sociology, American Studies, communication—these popular culture advocates lead double lives. In their curriculum vitae you will find an odd assortment of published papers, half on traditional topics within their respective disciplines and half on specialized topics dealing with popular art. Leisure time reading is all too often converted willy-nilly into leisure time scholarship. In the process, there now exists more thorough documentation of twentieth-century American popular culture than for any other period in history and for any other society.

Unfortunately, many of these popular culture "regulars" have never given much thought to methodology. For the most part, they have simply built upon the training they received in their particular discipline and used whatever methodology was at hand to examine popular art. New Critics do objective studies of Agatha Christie's style. Sociologists compare socioeconomic status with patterns of popular culture consumption. Mass communication specialists do content analysis of male heroes in *Playboy* magazine fiction.

Those who *are* interested in methodology are often advocates for a particular "revisionist" approach currently sweeping their discipline. When structuralism first became widely known in America in the mid-Seventies, a whole host of structuralists invaded the 1975 Popular Culture Association meeting in St. Louis determined to make structuralism the orthodox methodology for popular culture scholarship. To their dismay, they encountered a handful of rebels who advocated other alternatives, semiotics and the "new" hermeneutics.

My point here is not that structuralism or hermeneutic methods should not be applied to popular art products. They obviously make a useful contribution. I am merely observing that, in general, the study of popular culture has reached an uncomfortable stasis. The search for answers cannot move far forward because there are too many voices, too many separate interests, too many conflicting points of view.

I quickly add that Dramatism is not being promoted as the methodological end-all, be-all for popular art studies. If I were to suggest that it were, I could rightfully stand accused of being a hypocrite, condemning others for being too narrow in their application of particular methods and then doing the same. I do feel that Dramatism is the most comprehensive alternative yet put forward, not because it is *ex*clusive, but because it is *in*clusive of other approaches. Dramatism has timely application in popular art studies because it may help open up the discussion once again. Dramatism is praxeological, not ideological; generative, not reductionist. The beauty of Dramatism is that within its own borders it can encompass all the newer methods—structuralism, semiotics, the new hermeneutics.[3] In many ways, Dramatism is not a methodology *per se* but a *heuristic,* a generative model which enables us to ask a set of relevant questions on any topic.

The heuristic power of Dramatism has scarcely been demonstrated in the present study. The observations made in earlier chapters are simply a start. Many of the topics I have raised could be expanded into full-length studies; for example, the discussion of artistic collaboration in Chapter I could become the basis for a complete study of the creation of a single film or popular television program. A scholar writing on such a topic could begin to use sources of information frequently overlooked or ignored by those in academe: trade publications, personal interviews, diaries, corporate memos, annotated copies of shooting scripts, and the like.

Another useful study would be a comprehensive

comparison between Burke and Cawelti. Cawelti is obviously well-read in literary criticism, American Studies, and mass communication, but for some reason he seems ignorant of Burke. Nonetheless, his work focuses squarely on the complex dialectic between popular art and social custom, and throughout his writings he seems to be quite aware of the role of the symbol in transmitting ideas and values.[4] In this study, we have barely scratched the surface of the concept of popular formulae. These ideas definitely need to be taken further.

The Burkean concept of identification, a crucial component of audience response, ought to be compared with some of the psychological studies of literary response emanating from Norman N. Holland. Savor for a brief moment Holland's description of audience response, and you will discover the obvious relationship with Burke's ideas:

> The literary text provides us with a fantasy which we introject, experiencing it as though it were our own, supplying our own associations to it. The literary work manages this fantasy in two broad ways: by shaping it with formal devices which operate roughly like defenses; by transforming the fantasy toward ego-acceptable meanings—something like sublimation. The pleasure we experience is the feeling of having a fantasy of our own and our own associations to it managed and controlled but at the same time allowed a limited expression and gratification.[5]

Along with studies of the psychology of audience response, we might add response studies that integrate Dramatism with some of the current psycholinguistic research on reading theory and language acquisition. Is "learning a culture" via popular art similar to "learning a language"? This would be a fascinating point to pursue. Overall, I feel that Dramatistic studies of audience response would surely rescue us from the tedium of "quantitative" studies of audience behavior.

Much practical criticism remains to be done. The short sections on *Jaws, Shogun* and *The Dead Zone* in this volume are simply illustrative examples of what could be done with

Dramatism to explore specific aspects of works of popular art. It would be exciting to see Dramatism applied in a full-length study of some aspect of popular art, say an analysis of an individual genre or the career of a particular artist. The "definitive study" of the Harlequin Romance series of novels, for example, can and should be written from a Dramatistic perspective. So should a book on the writings of Mickey Spillane, or some other popular writer.

For its own part, the present study has reached its destination. With so many dreams to dream, and so much more to be done in the area of "applied Dramatism," I find it hard to disembark. The temptation is to stay on board and ride to the next city, hoping the conductor will fail to notice that my ticket is already punched. But he no doubt will notice. And like it or not, I must trust that the modest aims of this work have been fulfilled. Hopefully the many audiences to whom this study is addressed—students of Burke, students of popular culture, rhetoricians, literary critics, sociologists, mass communication scholars, Americanists and an assortment of curious onlookers—will all have found something of interest. Like most syntheses, the observations and conclusions in this volume are fragile and tentative at best. Their value may be better determined by the type of work that follows.

Notes

[1] Stanley Edgar Hyman, "Kenneth Burke and the Criticism of Symbolic Action" in *Critical Responses to Kenneth Burke: 1924-1966*, ed. William H. Rueckert (Minneapolis: Univ. of Minnesota Press, 1969), p. 213.

[2] Kenneth Burke, *Attitudes Toward History* (1937; rpt. Boston: Beacon Press, 1961), p. 196.

[3] See for example my comparison of Burke's methods with those employed by the new hermeneuticists, Hans Georg Gadamer in particular. C. Ronald Kimberling, "Kenneth Burke and the Rebirth of Hermeneutic Scholarship," in *Kenneth Burke in the Eighties: Where Are We Now?*, Southern California Occasional Papers in Rhetoric, No. I, ed. W. Ross Winterowd (Los Angeles: Univ. of Southern California Dept. of English,

forthcoming).

⁴See especially John G. Cawelti, "Literary Formulas and their Cultural Significance," in *The Study of American Culture: Contemporary Conflicts,* ed. Luther S. Luedtke (Deland, Florida: Everett/Edwards, 1977).

⁵Norman N. Holland, *The Dynamics of Literary Response* (New York: Oxford Univ. Press, 1968), pp. 311-12.

Bibliography

Burke, Kenneth. *Attitudes Toward History.* 1937; rpt. Boston: Beacon Press 1961.

_____. *Counter-Statement.* 1931; rpt. Berkeley: Univ. of California Press, 1968.

_____. "Dramatism." *International Encyclopedia of the Social Sciences.* ed. David L. Still. New York: The MacMillan Co. and The Free Press, 1968. Vol. VII.

_____. *A Grammar of Motives.* New York: Prentice-Hall, 1945.

_____. *Language as Symbolic Action: Essays on Life, Literature, and Method.* Berkeley: Univ. of California Press, 1966.

_____. *A Rhetoric of Motives.* 1950; rpt. Berkeley: Univ. of California Press, 1969.

Cain, Betty. "Kenneth Burke's Four Pentads." In *Kenneth Burke in the Eighties: Where Are We Now?* Southern California Occasional Papers in Rhetoric, No. I. ed. W. Ross Winterowd, Los Angeles: Univ. of Southern California Dept. of English, forthcoming.

Cawelti, John G. *Adventure, Mystery, and Romance: Formula Stories as Art and Popular Culture.* Chicago: Univ. of Chicago Press, 1976.

_____. "The Concept of Formula in the Study of Popular Literature." *Journal of Popular Culture,* 3 (1969), 381-90.

_____. "Literary Formulas and their Cultural Significance." In *The Study of American Culture: Contemporary Conflicts.* Ed Luther S. Luedtke. Deland, Florida: Everett/Edwards, 1977.

_____. "Myth, Symbol, and Formula." *Journal of Popular Culture,* 8 (1974), 1-9.

_____. "Notes Toward a Typology of Literary Formulas." *Indiana Social Studies Quarterly,* 26, No. 3 (1973-74), 21-34.

_____. "Notes Toward an Aesthetic of Popular Culture." *Journal of Popular Culture,* 5 (1971), 255-68.

_____. *The Six-Gun Mystique.* Bowling Green, Ohio: Bowling Green Univ. Popular Press, 1971.

Durgnat, Raymond. "Art and Audience." *British Journal of Aesthetics,* 10 (1970), 11-24.

Feehan, Michael George. "A Dramatistic Grammar of Literary Reception: Perspectives on 'Leaves of Grass.' " Diss. Univ. of Southern California, 1979.

Frye, Northrop. "Myth, Fiction, and Displacement." In *Fables of Identity.* New York: Harcourt Brace Jovanovich, 1963.

Gans, Herbert J. *Popular Culture and High Culture: An Analysis and Evaluation of Taste.* New York: Basic Books, 1974.

Gardner, Howard and Ellen Winner. "The Development of Metaphoric

Competence: Implications for Humanistic Disciplines." *Critical Inquiry,* 5 (1978), 123-41.

Getze, John. "Jaws Swims to the Top in Ocean of Publicity." *Los Angeles Times,* 28 Sept. 1975, Part 7, pp. 1-2.

Gottlieb, Carl. *The Jaws Log.* New York: Dell, 1975.

Hirsch, E.D. Jr. *Validity in Interpretation.* New Haven, Conn.: Yale Univ. Press, 1967.

Holland, Norman N. *The Dynamics of Literary Response.* New York: Oxford Univ. Press, 1968.

Hyman, Stanley Edgar. "Kenneth Burke and the Criticism of Symbolic Action." In *Critical Responses to Kenneth Burke: 1924-1966.* ed. William H. Rueckert. Minneapolis: Univ. of Minnesota Press, 1969.

Kaplan, Abraham. "The Aesthetics of the Popular Arts." In *Modern Culture and the Arts.* Ed. James B. Hall and Barry Ulanov. 2nd ed. New York: McGraw-Hill, 1967.

Kimberling, C. Ronald. "Kenneth Burke and the Rebirth of Hermeneutic Scholarship." In *Kenneth Burke in the Eighties: Where Are We Now?* Southern California Occasional Papers in Rhetoric, No. I. ed. W. Ross Winterowd. Los Angeles: Univ. of Southern California Dept. of English, forthcoming.

King, Stephen. *The Dead Zone.* New York: New American Library, 1979.

Mailloux, Steven John. "Interpretive Conventions and Recent Anglo-American Literary Theory." Diss. Univ. of Southern California, 1978.

McLuhan, Marshall. *Understanding Media: The Extensions of Man.* 1964; rpt. New York: McGraw-Hill, 1965.

Newcomb, Horace. *TV: The Most Popular Art.* Garden City, New York: Anchor Press/Doubleday, 1974.

Shils, Edward. "Mass Society and Its Culture." *Daedalus,* 89 (1960), 288-314.

Wimsatt, William K. Jr. and Monroe Beardsley. "The Intentional Fallacy." In *The Verbal Icon: Studies in the Meaning of Poetry.* Lexington, Kentucky: Univ. of Kentucky Press, 1954.

Winterowd, W. Ross. "Brain, Rhetoric, and Style." In *Linguistics, Stylistics, and the Teaching of Composition.* ed. Donald McQuade. Akron, Ohio: Univ. of Akron, 1979.

Index

105